P9-CIS-187

ALSO BY JEAN HERSEY

Flowering Shrubs and Small Trees
Cooking with Herbs
The Shape of a Year
A Sense of Seasons
The Woman's Day Book of House Plants
Wildflowers to Know and Grow
Carefree Gardening
Garden in Your Window
Halfway to Heaven
I Like Gardening

WITH ROBERT HERSEY

Change in the Wind
These Rich Years

The
Woman's Day
Book
of
WILDFLOWERS

BY

Jean Hersey

ILLUSTRATED BY

Fritz Kredel

SIMON AND SCHUSTER · NEW YORK

Copyright © 1960, 1976 by Fawcett Publications
All rights reserved
including the right of reproduction
in whole or in part in any form
Published by Simon and Schuster
A Gulf +Western Company
Rockefeller Center, 630 Fifth Avenue
New York, New York 10020
Designed by Edith Fowler
Manufactured in the United States of America
1   2   3   4   5   6   7   8   9   10

Library of Congress Cataloging in Publication Data

Hersey, Jean, date.
  The Woman's day book of wildflowers.

  Includes index.
  1. Wild flowers—United States—Identification.
2. Wild flowers—Canada—Identification.   3. Wild
flower gardening.   I. Title.
QK115.H44   1976   582'.13'0973   76-57
ISBN 0-671-22251-1

Acknowledgments

For knowledge and wisdom shared, I owe a debt of gratitude to many. I wish particularly to express thanks to Holly and Harvey Woltman for the use of their extensive library and to Fritzie Haugland for her general cooperation and her important help in research. Betty Frost's talent with Oshibana contributed greatly to my chapter on the decorative uses of wildflowers. Amy Christiansen, having an imaginative and magic touch with all dried flowers, was an inspiration and a very real aid as she shared her knowledge and experience. Dan Walden's enthusiasm, his botanical knowledge and his skillful and understanding editing assistance were all invaluable.

FOR BOB

With whom I have loved wandering
and exploring wilderness areas

Contents

Wild Magic

A woodland trail is a path to discovery and adventure into a new realm. The breeze stirs the Trout Lilies on the stream bank. Filtered sun dances over their jaunty golden petals. Clean-cut but crowded leaves of wild Lily-of-the-valley stand near. On the bank beside the rocks a few Hepatica plants lift fresh blue blossoms dusted with white stamens from a bed of last year's rusty leaves. Christmas Ferns rise out of the earth in clusters of silver-white buttonhooks. In the shallows Skunk Cabbage unwinds its shell-like forms.

A quiet theme this, a refreshing, renewing scene. Backgrounding the beauty of the wildflowers are the sounds and rhythms of nature. The breeze moves plants, the stream murmurs, you watch the weaving of five trout in the watery depths below an old stump there. You listen to a rustle somewhere in a branch above. A bird calls and feathery wings carry him off. In the leaves at your feet the faintest, fastest sound, and a small orange lizard darts behind a pine cone. You are but a visitor in this woods where worlds penetrate worlds. If you whisper and move gently, can you keep from being an intruder? Quietly you breathe in the beauty, the tranquility. For a few moments you merge with it. You are one with the golden Lilies blowing, the bird that winged away, the lizard darting over wet brown leaves, the rhythm of the weaving trout.

A world of wildflowers is vast and exciting. Here is nature unobstructed. Here no hand of man has planned or fashioned that sweep of snowy Starflowers, those Marsh Marigolds in the swamp or that ledge of Trailing Arbutus above the path. In nature's private sanctuary man is never master or teacher but always student and learner. The long passageways of laurel and rhododendron in the Smokies, with their tall upreaching limbs, are like the vaulted aisles of European cathedrals. You pause in wonder and awe. What stillness is here! And a kind of solitude that is never loneliness. What you see, what you feel, stirs and quickens your own deep centers and touches your depths.

A grove of dogwoods and silverbell trees in full flower creates a different mood and starts your spirits dancing. I have stood hypnotized before a mountainside of nodding white Trillium in the Blue Ridge Mountains. I have felt my spine tingle with joy and excitement driving across the plains of Texas where Bluebonnets reached the horizon on all sides. What magic lay in that locust grove on Cape Cod one fresh June day, with blankets of blue Lupine folding everywhere over the earth.

There was an afternoon in a meadow of Daisies, stretching out lazily on the warm earth. As far as we could see, Daisies—white Daisies with yellow centers against the blue sky. Another time, another scene: a clear October morning—the sea was blue, the sky was blue, the sand was white, everywhere spires of Goldenrod were bending in the breeze.

Wildflowers are nature on her own terms, a realm where man is humbled in a healthy manner. Who of us but is moved to bow in reverence before that spread of stately pink Lady's-slipper under the pines? Wildflowers are a constant surprise. You never know what you will come upon around the next bend, over the next dune or just beyond that wooded copse.

These are the plants whose lives prove no man-made theories or concepts. They bloom to bloom, they give their beauty, their fragrance, their nectar, just to give. They form seeds and spread, create and re-create, merely to be. So much of our lives is focused and directed to worldly ends. Not that there is anything wrong with worldly goals and directions. Mankind and civilization need both. But it's also good to be aware of aims different from those of man. It is revitalizing to touch a world where purposes involve being rather than doing or achieving.

How uncluttered and simple is the life of a wildflower—unorganized, unplanned, unstructured in the human sense. As part of a larger destiny, these plants have much to tell us when we pause, when we look and when we listen.

We are the roadside flowers,
Straying from garden grounds,—
Lovers of idle hours,
Breakers of ordered bounds.

BLISS CARMAN

Part One

200 WILDFLOWERS
TO IDENTIFY

200 Wildflowers

The fragile Windflower is beautiful as you study a delicate bloom, whether or not you know its name. But there is also pleasure and satisfaction in learning not only the name but a little about the plant. Why the name Windflower? Legend tells us that its original home was Mt. Olympus, home of the gods, where winds forever blow.

While admiring creamy white flowers in casual clusters, it is fascinating to learn that they are called New Jersey tea and that American soldiers boiled the foliage and drank the brew in Revolutionary times when real tea was difficult to get.

In other words, it is provocative and exciting to be able to identify wildflowers—to know their names and a little bit about them.

The simplest way to identify a wildflower is by color and season of bloom. This book divides two hundred of the more common varieties into four color groups, each broken down according to the time the blossoms appear. The four color groups are (1) white, variable and off-white, green tints; (2) clear blue, lavender and purple; (3) yellow, orange-yellow and orange; (4) pink, purple-red and red. Seasons of bloom are spring (March, April, May); summer (June, July, August); fall (September, October, November). The color breakdown is a little arbitrary, since variables such as soil nutrients and climate alter color from one region to another, and even within the same few miles the quality of the earth varies and tones may be different. The Gentians are deeper in color in high altitudes and under mountain conditions than they are in a low field. Wild Columbine shades may be stronger a few miles up the hill than down in the valley. There are also variables in season of bloom. Spring comes earlier in some parts of the country than in others, and there may be a considerable time overlap in the appearance of some of the late summer and early fall flowers. Daisies bloom in early May in North Carolina and in June on Cape Cod.

Here is how you use the book. Suppose on an early spring day you are walking in the woods and wonder about a white flower you discover. What kind is it? It is like a Daisy, but not really, because the petals are too long and the plant too low. Turn to the section on white flowers. Then, because it is early spring, leaf through the beginning of the section. Presently you find an illustration of the very flower that puzzled you. It is Bloodroot, the second in the book and one of the earliest of all to flower.

Or possibly on an October day you are walking along a dirt road and here in part shade is a whole clump of flowers blue as the sky above. Each one has four fringed petals. What can it be? To identify turn to the "blue" section and toward the end because it is a fall flower. And there, in the illustration, you see the same blossom and recognize it as the Fringed Gentian.

You will also be able to use this part of the book to help you plant and grow wildflowers on your own land. In the several categories included in each caption, you are given hints and specific instructions on the location where a plant will grow best, the kind of soil needed, the time to transplant, ways to propagate, the range in which it is found, whether it is easy or difficult to grow. You will also learn a bit of beguiling history, perhaps where the plant came from originally; occasionally some old-time lore or facts will enlighten you about its ancient uses.

Some varieties are adaptable to different soils, but many prefer or must have acid or alkaline soil. You can get a soil-testing kit to learn just which your earth is on different parts of your grounds. This is a good guide to aid you in knowing where to put the different wild plants.

Each caption contains the comments "Do pick," "May pick" or "Don't pick." These suggestions are based on whether or not the flower is protected by conservation laws or whether the blooms wilt so fast there is no advantage to picking. Also, picking flowers causes harm to certain plants—sometimes this is the reason for the "Don't pick."

BEARBERRY (*Arctostaphylos uva-ursi*). Heath Family
At every season mats of green, thick and bouncy to walk on, spill over the great rolling hills of Truro on Cape Cod. In spring diminutive waxy urn-shaped flowers peek from clusters of firm, dark evergreen leaves. The trailing plants are of a shrubby nature with stems that are ruddy and hairy-rough. Decorative red berries appear in autumn, lasting for months. In the Northwest it is also called Kinikinick, its Indian name.

COLOR: Pink-tipped white flowers.

HEIGHT: 6 inches.

SEASON OF BLOOM: Spring.

LOCATION: Flourishes in dry meadows; spreads over sandy banks, dunes and swales; grows along roadsides and stone walls; fringes pine and oak woodlands; trails down hillsides.

SOIL: Poor sandy earth; not necessarily, but often, acid.

TRANSPLANTING TIME: Early spring or fall. Very difficult.

PROPAGATION: By division and separation of roots. You can also plant berries an inch under the soil (but germination may take two years). Much better to purchase plants in peat pots and bury pot and plant.

DON'T PICK.

RANGE: Eastern states, Yellowstone Park, Montana, Canadian Rockies, Northwest, California.

BLOODROOT (*Sanguinaria canadensis*). Poppy Family
Bloodroot is a special spring delight. The flowers drift through open woodlands, emerging from carpets of many seasons' crumbling dry leaves. Bruise or break a root and it bleeds red. The red sap was used as an ancient Indian cough remedy and also as a dye. Best of all are the snowy-white blossoms. Seven or eight narrow tapering petals surround a center of golden stamens and open flat in the morning. Then the flowers resemble miniature water lilies afloat on a forest floor of old leaves. By midafternoon the petals rise up and at dusk they gradually fold. Next morning the bloom is again open and wide-eyed. Each plant has one large gray-green scalloped leaf.

COLOR: White.

HEIGHT: To 10 inches.

SEASON OF BLOOM: Early spring.

LOCATION: Western slopes preferred. Flourishes near field stones and rocks and along stone walls. Must have partial or deep shade, average moisture and a winter cover of leaves—oak or beech are best. Often found bordering shady back roads.

SOIL: Adaptable. Does well in rich, damp, neutral or slightly acid soil.

TRANSPLANTING TIME: Early fall when the plants are single stalks topped by umbrella-like green leaves.

PROPAGATION: Seed. Sow in sifted woodland soil as soon as seeds are ripe. Germinates the following spring and blooms one year later.

DON'T PICK. Doing so harms the plant.

RANGE: Southern Canada, Maine to North Carolina, west to Minnesota and Kansas.

FALSE SOLOMON'S-SEAL (*Smila-cina racemosa*). Lily Family

Slim light-green leaves appear alternately up an arching stem. At the top a cluster of white foamy blossoms emerges. In autumn the leaves turn golden chartreuse. Above them the lacy florets, now transformed into a bunch of ruby-red berries (or sometimes paler red and speckled), provide a bright accent. A sweep of these flowers is stunning along the wandering gray-stone walls of New England. They also flourish in dim shadows beneath tall trees where they seem to sparkle on a dull day.

COLOR: White.

HEIGHT: 1 to 3 feet.

SEASON OF BLOOM: Spring.

LOCATION: High and low woodlands bordering roadsides in filtered sunlight. On the north or west side of stone walls.

SOIL: Acid.

TRANSPLANTING TIME: Early spring or fall.

PROPAGATION: Seed.

DON'T PICK.

RANGE: Eastern and Central states and Canada, with a closely related species in the West and Northwest.

DUTCHMAN'S-BREECHES

(*Dicentra cucullaria*). Fumitory Family

Three to seven two-spurred florets swinging along an arching tawny stalk suggest small-scale Dutch pantaloons hung on the clothesline. In the slightest zephyr they sway charmingly, carrying out the illusion. Every blossom is tipped with gold. Delicate stems emerge from feathery fernlike leaves to greet the spring. The foliage is as lovely as the flowers. Their botanical name, from the Greek, means "twice-spurred." Blooms are fertilized by early bees and other small insects.

COLOR: White tipped with gold.

HEIGHT: 5 to 9 inches.

SEASON OF BLOOM: Spring.

LOCATION: Found on the north slopes of partly shaded stream banks. In rich woods, both in mountains and low country. Are happiest on rocky banks.

SOIL: Acid or neutral, plenty of humus.

TRANSPLANTING TIME: Early, early spring. Take plenty of soil and disturb roots as little as possible.

PROPAGATION: By offsets from the corm.

DON'T PICK.

RANGE: Nova Scotia to North Carolina and west to Kansas.

FOAMFLOWER, MITERWORT

(Tiarella cordifolia). Saxifrage Family
In low woods and along shady brooksides drifts of these snowy flowers
flourish. Each one rises, a little feathery
plume, among the heart-shaped leaves.
Mature plants form large clumps with
many blossoming stalks. They spread
countless runners that soon root and
may be cut from the parent and moved
to a different location. The foliage turns
an interesting bronze in autumn. Observe the small seed capsule, characteristically cloven like a tiara. From this
the plant draws its name.

COLOR: White.
HEIGHT: 6 to 12 inches.
SEASON OF BLOOM: Spring.
LOCATION: Low woodlands and
shady stream banks, along forest trails.
SOIL: Acid to neutral, peaty.
TRANSPLANTING TIME: Spring or
fall, or summer during a rainy spell.
PROPAGATION: Multiplies readily
from newly rooted runners.
FRAGRANT. Scent most evident at
noon.
DON'T PICK.
RANGE: Canada to Georgia and
west to North Central states.

LARGE-FLOWERING TRILLIUM

(Trillium grandiflorum). Lily Family
Thrives in rich woods, in the mountains
or lowlands, where it grows in large
colonies. The pure white three-petaled
blossoms, each with three sepals, are
delicately ribbed and turn soft pink as
they age. Three leaves, sharply pointed,
form a green cushion for every flower.
I've seen great stands of these flowers
growing wild along the roadsides
throughout Ohio and Indiana. Here is
a plant of surprises that can break all
rules. While alleged to prefer shady
areas, we once grew a single robust
Trillium in our sunny Connecticut
perennial border. For years it flourished
and spread.

COLOR: White, turning to pink
with age.
HEIGHT: 7 to 15 inches.
SEASON OF BLOOM: Spring.
LOCATION: Filtered shade in open
woodlands. Sometimes adaptable to
other locations: do experiment.
SOIL: Acid to neutral.
TRANSPLANTING TIME: Early
spring or fall. Can also be moved when
blooming if you dig deep, take ample
earth, and don't disturb the roots.
PROPAGATION: Seed.
DON'T PICK.
RANGE: Quebec to North Caro-
lina and uplands of Missouri.

SOLOMON'S-SEAL (*Polygonatum biflorum*). Lily Family
Twin bell-like blossoms, small and flaring at the mouth, with united white petals, swing beneath every leaf. These leaves, oval and gracefully lined, appear alternately up a smooth and arching stem. By fall, the small flowers have ripened into pairs of blue-black berries that enhance the plant. Early Greek writers, finding the thick white roots with marks on them resembling the stamp of a seal, gave the plant its name. Gerarde, the famed herbalist, comments that these roots, crushed, cure bruises of all sorts, especially those gotten by "women's wilfulnesse in stumbling on their hasty husbands' fists or such like."
COLOR: Greenish-white.
HEIGHT: 1 to 3 feet.
SEASON OF BLOOM: Spring.
LOCATION: Plants usually grow in groups, clustering along stone walls through high, dry deciduous woodlands and clearings. Also in thickets and on hillsides.
SOIL: Acid to neutral.
TRANSPLANTING TIME: Spring or fall.
PROPAGATION: Seed.
DON'T PICK.
RANGE: New Brunswick to Tennessee, and westward to Iowa.

SWEET WHITE VIOLET (*Viola blanda*). Violet Family
A subtle fragrance in the woodland draws you to the small exquisite flower. Examine with a magnifier to better appreciate the graceful flower shapes and rhythmic markings. Young heart-shaped leaves are tender and delicious in spring salads. To surprise a special luncheon guest, try a few petals with watercress in white-bread sandwiches. They are delectable and unique. Viola is a name some say comes from the ancient Romans. These flowers bordered so many of their thoroughfares that they might have had *via* in mind. I rather like to envision the Romans of long ago clad in togas making their way through paths of violets.
COLOR: White with purple-veined petals.
HEIGHT: 3 to 5 inches.
SEASON OF BLOOM: Early spring.
LOCATION: Adaptable. Light shade, woodland stream banks, boggy or high dry areas, wet meadows and full sun.
SOIL: Adaptable. Acid or alkaline, light or heavy.
TRANSPLANTING TIME: Spring or fall best, but can be moved any time, particularly during a summer rainy spell.
PROPAGATION: Seed; division of roots.
FRAGRANT.
MAY PICK. Tiny bouquets in diminutive vases are charming.
RANGE: Quebec to Georgia and Louisiana. Also in Minnesota, Wyoming and California.

TOOTHWORT, CRINKLE-ROOT,
PEPPER-ROOT (*Dentaria diphylla*).
Mustard Family
On the white rootstock are toothlike
projections. It was an old-time country
belief that the root, when eaten, cured
toothaches. It has a slightly watercress
or pepper flavor and is an interesting
addition, diced, to salads. A cluster of
flowers emerges on a single stalk from,
usually, two opposite notched three-
lobed leaves. The dainty blooms are
waxy white and four-petaled, with many
gold stamens.
 COLOR: White petals with yellow
stamens.
 HEIGHT: 8 to 13 inches.
 SEASON OF BLOOM: Spring.
 LOCATION: Along shady brooksides, in rich woods and sunny bogs.
Along roadsides.
 SOIL: Acid, sandy or light leafy.
 TRANSPLANTING TIME: Spring or
fall, or during summer rainy spells.
 PROPAGATION: Seed; division of
rootstock.
 DON'T PICK.
 RANGE: Nova Scotia to South
Carolina and west to Minnesota.

WILD LILY-OF-THE-VALLEY
(*Maianthemum canadense*). Lily Family
The botanical name comes from Greek
mythology, To Maia, mother of
Hermes, the month of May was dedi-
cated. This delicate beauty was named
for the goddess and also for the month
of May, when it blooms. Many little
plants form a glossy green carpet set
with small flowers in upright racemes.
White berries following the flowers turn
in fall to a dull ruby red.
 COLOR: White.
 HEIGHT: 3 to 6 inches.
 SEASON OF BLOOM: Spring.
 LOCATION: Above rocky outcrop-
pings, by shady brooksides, in the
shadows of moist woodland vales.
 SOIL: Acid.
 TRANSPLANTING TIME: Fall.
 PROPAGATION: Seed, cuttings.
 DON'T PICK.
 RANGE: Newfoundland to North
Carolina and west to South Dakota.

YARROW, MILFOIL (*Achillea millefolium*). Daisy Family

The Latin name is in honor of Achilles, who found the plant useful in promoting the healing of wounds in the Trojan War. The soldiers first ground the leaves, steeped them in boiling water and applied them to wounds; also to bruises and burns—for which the plant is still useful today. The American Indians followed the same procedure. The plant is an import from Europe. All across the United States you now find this gray-green feathery Yarrow. The blossom is composed of myriads of minute florets all pressed together in tight flat-topped clusters two to three inches broad.

COLOR: White or pink.

HEIGHT: 1 to 2 feet.

SEASON OF BLOOM: Early summer to September.

LOCATION: Woodlands, dry meadows, along roadsides. Does well in hot, arid pastures and beside dusty trails and roads. Impervious to drought and poor soil.

SOIL: Adaptable. Grows in the worst gravelly sandbanks.

TRANSPLANTING TIME: Spring or early fall.

PROPAGATION: Seed; division of root clumps; stem cuttings close to the ground will root.

FOLIAGE AROMATIC.

MAY PICK.

RANGE: Across the continent.

WOOD ANEMONE, WIND-FLOWER (*Anemone quinquefolia*). Buttercup Family

Legend says that this flower's original home was the Mountain of the Gods, Mount Olympus, where the wind almost always blows. The ancients believed that the blossom would not unfold unless blown by the breezes. Foliage and bloom are so frail and gossamer that the slightest zephyr stirs them. A solitary flower, perhaps an inch across, rises above deep-green leaves, each with five divisions. Grows by the thousands on the slopes of the Rocky Mountains, and less abundantly in the Northeastern woods.

COLOR: White sepals that appear to be petals surround a center of golden stamens.

HEIGHT: 6 to 12 inches.

SEASON OF BLOOM: Spring.

LOCATION: Open woodland, along brooksides, beneath deciduous trees, borders of forests.

SOIL: Definitely acid.

TRANSPLANTING TIME: Early spring or autumn.

PROPAGATION: Seed, crown divisions.

DON'T PICK.

RANGE: Southern Canada and Maine to Georgia, and in cooler areas across the United States to eastern Oregon and Washington. The Western form is slightly different, sometimes pale pink or pale blue.

BUNCHBERRY (*Cornus canadensis*).
Dogwood Family
A relative of the dogwood with rather
similar, though smaller, white-bracted
flowers, and more pointed leaves in a
whorl below the flower. Grows in dense
colonies as a groundcover—an amazingly
beautiful one. The plant produces
clusters of scarlet berries in late summer.
These are edible, though slightly tart.
Quite good in a pudding with sugar and
lemon (after the seeds are strained out).
 COLOR: White.
 HEIGHT: 3 to 8 inches.
 SEASON OF BLOOM: Spring and
summer.
 LOCATION: Along brooksides, in
thickets and cool mountain woods.
 SOIL: Acid.
 TRANSPLANTING TIME: Spring or
fall.
 PROPAGATION: Seed; division.
Difficult.
 DON'T PICK.
 RANGE: Quebec to Alaska, south
in mountains to West Virginia. Also in
the northern Sierras of California.

FIELD CHICKWEED (*Cerastium
arvense*). Pink Family
An attractive low-growing, rather large-
flowered species of the common Chick-
weed. The broad white petals are deeply
cleft. Seeds develop in a thoroughly
fascinating horn-shaped capsule. These
are relished by birds and poultry, as the
common name suggests.
 COLOR: White.
 HEIGHT: 4 to 10 inches.
 SEASON OF BLOOM: Early summer.
 LOCATION: Sunny banks, hot dry
pastures and stony ground.
 SOIL: Acid.
 TRANSPLANTING TIME: Spring or
fall.
 PROPAGATION: Seed; cuttings;
separation of old plants. Spreads rapidly.
 MAY PICK.
 RANGE: Canada and across our
Northern states.

GOLDTHREAD (*Coptis trifolia*).
Buttercup Family
From amidst shiny deckle-edged leaves
emerge diminutive flowers with white,
pointed sepals that most people think
are petals. In the center of these are
found obscure club-shaped petals and
numerous white stamens with gold
anthers. The strange petals are actually
nectaries to feed thirsty insects. The
blossom is a subject for a close look
with a magnifier because of its exquisite
structure. The plant derives its name
from the roots' resemblance to yellow
threads. These are bitter but beneficial
medicinally—according to the old-time
country housewife.
    COLOR: White.
    HEIGHT: 3 to 6 inches.
    SEASON OF BLOOM: Early summer.
    LOCATION: Bogs and low wood-
lands, shady brooksides.
    SOIL: Acid, peaty.
    TRANSPLANTING TIME: Early
spring or fall.
    PROPAGATION: Seed; division of
plants.
    DON'T PICK.
    RANGE: A really northern plant,
Labrador to Alaska, but south in
Appalachians to Tennessee.

GROUNDNUT, DWARF GINSENG
(*Panax trifolium*). Ginseng Family
One of the popular names is from the
Chinese *Jin-chen*, or "manlike," for it
has a strange, two-legged root. Also,

according to many Oriental people, this
root possesses potent medicinal power.
It is somewhat rare, but is found in
northern woodlands. The globe-like
flower, rising above the foliage, is composed of countless minuscule florets.
Later in the season deep ruby-red
berries form in a scattered cluster.
    COLOR: White.
    HEIGHT: 3 to 6 inches.
    SEASON OF BLOOM: Early summer.
    LOCATION: Shaded woods and
along brooksides.
    SOIL: Acid to neutral.
    TRANSPLANTING TIME: Early
spring.
    PROPAGATION: Seed.
    FRAGRANT (suggestive of Lily-of-
the-valley.)
    MAY PICK.
    RANGE: Southeast Canada to
Georgia and west to Wisconsin.

**INDIAN POKE, FALSE OR
AMERICAN WHITE HELLEBORE**
(*Veratrum viride*). Lily Family
The lined and pleated pale-green leaves
are one of the woodlands' loveliest
spring sights. They rapidly grow up to
twelve inches long and six inches wide.
Roots and foliage are poisonous to
sheep and cattle. Small insignificant
greenish-white flowers grow up a
number of single green stems at the
top of the plant. The beautiful spring
foliage is a pure yellow-green and far
lovelier than the flower. But keep your
distance.
    COLOR: Greenish white.
    HEIGHT: 2 to 7 feet.

SEASON OF BLOOM: Early summer.
LOCATION: Along stream banks, in swamps, sunny bogs, wet woods.
SOIL: Acid.
TRANSPLANTING TIME: Spring or fall.
PROPAGATION: Seed; lifting and dividing clumps.
DON'T PICK.
RANGE: New Brunswick to Georgia, and west to Minnesota.

MARSH TREFOIL, BOGBEAN, BUCKBEAN (*Menyanthes trifoliata*). Gentian Family

A snowflake imprisoned in a flower! Many small florets open in succession up a straight stiff stalk. As the petals unfold, with a magnifying glass you can observe miniature feathery flower parts along with brown stamens. The inside of the petals is fringed with frosty hairs. The last blossoms to unfold are those at the top of the stem. In bud they are a delicate shell pink. Light-green lined leaves are three-lobed.

COLOR: White.
HEIGHT: 10 inches.
SEASON OF BLOOM: Early summer.
LOCATION: In sunny bogs, by ponds, lakes and streams, often standing in water.
SOIL: Acid.
TRANSPLANTING TIME: Spring or early fall.
PROPAGATION: Insertion of shoots into mudbanks.
DON'T PICK.
RANGE: Northern half of United States from east to west, and in Canada.

NEW JERSEY TEA (*Ceanothus americanus*). Buckthorn Family

In Revolutionary times, when tea was scarce or nonexistent, American soldiers brewed the foliage of this wild plant for their beverage. Stems are brown-green or bronzy, leaves dull green, pointed and very finely toothed. Creamy-white flowers are borne in casual feathery clusters from the joint between leaf and main stem.

COLOR: White.
HEIGHT: 1 to 4 feet.
SEASON OF BLOOM: Spring and summer.
LOCATION: Dry open woodlands, high fields, along stone walls.
SOIL: Acid to neutral.
TRANSPLANTING TIME: Early fall.
PROPAGATION: Cuttings.
FRAGRANT. A subtle, gentle scent.
MAY PICK.
RANGE: Maine to South Carolina and west to Texas.

PARTRIDGE BERRY, TWIN-
BERRY (*Mitchella repens*). Madder
Family
Oval pink buds, often in pairs, open
into very small twin flowers, each one a
little star. Low growing; hugs the earth.
Streamers of round, shiny, green-
leaved stems carpet the soil, forming a
delightful groundcover. In autumn and
on through the winter the plant is
covered with bright red berries. Two or
three scarlet-berried stems will be a
feature in your terrarium. Grow your
own for picking each Christmastime.
Wild partridges relish the berries.
American Indian women, before giving
birth, drank tea made from the foliage
to ease delivery.

COLOR: Pinkish-white.
HEIGHT: 2 to 5 inches, trailing.
SEASON OF BLOOM: Early sum-
mer.
LOCATION: Deep woods, mossy
areas, under evergreen trees, along
forest banks.
SOIL: Acid.
TRANSPLANTING TIME: Spring.
PROPAGATION: Seed; long runners
root and can be separated from parent
plant.
DON'T PICK.
RANGE: Newfoundland to Minne-
sota, south to Florida and Texas.

RED BANEBERRY (*Actaea rubra*).
Buttercup Family
The panicles of bloom are slightly
domed. The many stamens are more
conspicuous than the petals, and are
soft as white fur to the touch. Compound three- to five-part leaves are
toothed in a casual, raggedy manner. In
autumn coral-red berries develop; they
are poisonous if eaten. Fertilized by
small bees.

COLOR: White.
HEIGHT: 1 to 2 feet.
SEASON OF BLOOM: Spring and
summer.
LOCATION: Thickets, dry wood-
lands, shaded banks.
SOIL: Acid to neutral.
TRANSPLANTING TIME: Spring or
early fall.

PROPAGATION: Seed; lifting and
separating clumps.
MAY PICK.
RANGE: Labrador to New Jersey
and westward to eastern Washington.

STARFLOWER (*Trientalis americana* or *borealis*). Primrose Family
Five to nine lance-shaped pointed light-
green leaves, tapering at both ends,
radiate from the tip of a seven-inch
stem. From the center rise two slender
threadlike stalks, each bearing a fragile,
starry bloom. The long delicate stamens
are tipped by tiny gold anthers. Grows
in the northern part of the country, as
is suggested by *borealis*, and is most
effective in large dense patches.

COLOR: White.
HEIGHT: 3 to 7 inches.
SEASON OF BLOOM: Spring and
summer.

LOCATION: In moist thickets and woods, along shady brooks.
SOIL: Acid.
TRANSPLANTING TIME: Early spring or fall.
PROPAGATION: Seed; division of roots.
DON'T PICK.
RANGE: Eastern Canada, north-eastern and north central United States.

WESTERN EVENING PRIMROSE (*Oenthera albicaulis*). Evening Prim-rose Family
Great patches of lovely fragrant flowers drift over the sandy western prairies from Montana and the Dakotas to New Mexico. They suggest the great white single wild roses found on the Cape Cod beaches, except that the petals are slightly cupped. Branching stems are whitish and downy with shredding bark. Foliage is sea-green and toothed. Red-tinted buds open to white blossoms, which after pollination turn gradually pink, then crimson.
COLOR: White changing to pink.
HEIGHT: To 2 feet.
SEASON OF BLOOM: Spring and summer.
LOCATION: Dry hot open sunny fields. Sandy places, prairies.
SOIL: Gravelly sandy soil. Adaptable.
TRANSPLANTING TIME: Early spring or late fall.
PROPAGATION: Seed.
FRAGRANT.
DON'T PICK.
RANGE: See descriptive paragraph above.

WOOD SORREL (*Oxalis acetosella*). Geranium Family
Charming flower found also in Europe and Japan. The name, from the Greek, means "sharply acid" and refers to the taste of the foliage. This may be used in a salad for an interesting flavor, but in moderation because of the oxalic acid contained. Each leaf is composed of three green hearts joined at the top of the stem. At night and in rain these fold together. The frail flowers are deli-cate and gentle, and appear by the thousands on the floor of northern forests.
COLOR: White, pink-veined.
HEIGHT: 3 to 4 inches.
SEASON OF BLOOM: Spring and summer.
LOCATION: Cool, damp woods and edge of streams. A forest plant.
SOIL: Adaptable; acid or slightly so.
TRANSPLANTING TIME: Spring or fall.
PROPAGATION: Seed; runners.
FRAGRANT. The scent is the essence of spring.
DON'T PICK.
RANGE: Introduced from Europe to northern parts of the United States and southern Canada.

OUR LORD'S CANDLE (*Hespero-yucca whipplei*). Lily Family
From amongst blue-green foliage, fierce and sharp, rises a great shaft of hundreds of waxy white blossoms. In the West this may be seen from a great distance; it towers up to fifteen feet, a giant candle on the mountainside. A truly noble plant that is at its best in California and Arizona. The closely related Yucca (various kinds), or Spanish Bayonet, is the state flower of New Mexico. Fibers from the foliage of both were widely used by the Indians.
COLOR: Waxy cream-colored.
HEIGHT: 5 to 15 feet.
SEASON OF BLOOM: Summer.
LOCATION: Dry hot sandy open meadows, mountainsides, steep banks.
SOIL: Gravelly, rough, poor soil.
TRANSPLANTING TIME: Spring.
PROPAGATION: Suckers; offsets; cuttings.
DON'T PICK.
RANGE: Southern California, Arizona.

AMERICAN LOTUS, SACRED BEAN (*Nelumbium luteum*). Water Lily Family
The leaves of this aquatic plant, sometimes two feet across, are a fine sunning spot for frogs and a landing field for dragonflies. Stems rise up above the water surface to bear their glorious exotic blossoms aloft. As the petals fall, the gold center of the bloom changes gradually into a firm cone-shaped seed-pod as exciting and decorative as the flowers. Watch drops of water slide silver across the foliage. Indians relish the tubers. When baked they taste like sweet potatoes. Primitive people also boiled and roasted the immature seeds that are flavored like chestnuts.
COLOR: White with gold centers.
HEIGHT: Grows to 2 feet above shallow water.
SEASON OF BLOOM: Summer.
LOCATION: Ponds, rivers, lakes.
SOIL: Swampy muck and bottom of shallow water.
TRANSPLANTING TIME: Late spring.
PROPAGATION: Seed; division of tubers.
FRAGRANT. A clean, fresh scent.
MAY PICK.
RANGE: Southern Ontario to Florida and Louisiana. More abundant in the South.

BEACH CLOTBUR *(Xanthium echinatum)*. Daisy Family
The plant that travels! Interesting spiny green burs with two clawlike hooks cling to clothing and thus are carried to new places to grow. Named from the German *klette* meaning "to stick," and the English bur that adheres to hair and clothing.

COLOR: Insignificant greenish flowers without petals.

HEIGHT: 1 to 2 feet.

SEASON OF BLOOM: Summer.

LOCATION: Beaches, lake shores, sand dunes, bluffs.

SOIL: Sandy, gravelly, light soil, sometimes clayey.

TRANSPLANTING TIME: Spring.

PROPAGATION: Sow seed when ripe in late summer or fall.

DON'T PICK.

RANGE: Maine to North Carolina and westward to North Dakota.

BEARDTONGUE, PENSTEMON *(Penstemon hirsutus)*. Snapdragon Family
In summer this delightful plant opens many blossoms all the way up a slim stalk, beginning to unfold at the bottom. Leaves are slim and pointed and grow in pairs opposite each other the length of the stem. Invites a host of gay and colorful butterflies to fertilize it. The meadow where it grows will be alive with a variety of these colorful beauties.

COLOR: White tinged with dull magenta.

HEIGHT: 2 feet.

SEASON OF BLOOM: Summer.

LOCATION: Dry meadows, thickets, woodland fringes, rocky banks.

SOIL: Adaptable. Makes a good garden plant.

TRANSPLANTING TIME: Spring. Very easy. Keep moist several days after moving.

PROPAGATION: Seed or cuttings; self-sows readily.

MAY PICK.

RANGE: Maine to Georgia and Midwest.

BLADDER CAMPION, WHITE VEIN *(Silene cucubalus)*. Pink Family
Originally from Europe, but now naturalized throughout much of the country. Five snowy petals with ten anthers emerge from a soft magenta melon-shaped cup. These globes are interestingly veined and patterned. The name Campion comes from the Latin *campus* (field), where the plant usually grows.

COLOR: White, occasionally pinkish.

HEIGHT: 6 to 24 inches.

SEASON OF BLOOM: Summer.

LOCATION: Dry fields, sunny wet meadows, waste places, along roadsides.

SOIL: Poor soil—clay or sandy. An adaptable plant.

TRANSPLANTING TIME: Early spring or fall.

PROPAGATION: Seed; cuttings; division.

MAY PICK.

RANGE: Maine to Iowa and Arkansas and westward.

BUTTONBUSH, BUSH GLOBE-
FLOWER (*Cephalanthus occidentalis*).
Madder Family
The pincushion flower. A globular head
of florets appears to be stuck with
countless yellow-tipped pins (anthers).
The blossoms turn to hard ball-like
seedpods, the cores of which were once
used as buttons—hence the name.
> COLOR: White.
> HEIGHT: 3 to 10 feet. A shrub.
> SEASON OF BLOOM: Summer to
early fall.
> LOCATION: Swamps, shallow
water, low ground along lakes and
streams.
> SOIL: Acid.
> TRANSPLANTING TIME: Summer
and fall.
> PROPAGATION: Seed; cuttings.
> FRAGRANT. Like jasmine, but
fainter.
> MAY PICK.
> RANGE: Swamps across North
America.

HEDGE BINDWEED (*Convolvulus
sepium*). Morning-glory Family
A flower that greets the dawn and
closes by noon. From amongst arrow-
shaped gray-green leaves on a climbing
or trailing plant emerge countless bell-
like white flowers, each with a rosy
tinge. Note how the buds are attractively furled. A newly opened bloom is
delicate as tissue paper.
> COLOR: White, pink-tinted.
> HEIGHT: 3 to 10 feet, a vine.
> SEASON OF BLOOM: Summer.
> LOCATION: Moist areas along
roadsides, in fields, thickets.
> SOIL: Neutral and not too rich.
> TRANSPLANTING TIME: Spring.
> PROPAGATION: Seed. Can become
a pervasive weed.
> DON'T PICK.
> RANGE: Newfoundland to Cali-
fornia, and widespread in many parts
of the world.

INDIAN PIPE (*Monotropa uniflora*).
Shinleaf Family
A relative of the rhododendron. Waxy-
white ghostly blossoms push up through
thick pine needles or dead oak leaves in
deep and dim forest shadows. Wilts
immediately when exposed to sunlight.
The plant is weirdly leafless except for
the scaly bracts clinging up the flower
stalk. Blossom head grows in a nodding
position, creating the effect of a meer-
schaum pipe in miniature. The Indians
used an extract of the plant for eye
irritations.
> COLOR: White.
> HEIGHT: 3 to 9 inches.
> SEASON OF BLOOM: Summer in
northern states, November to December
in deep South.
> LOCATION: Moist, rich forest
depths, among oak or pine trees.
Thrives among decaying vegetation.
> SOIL: Acid.

TRANSPLANTING TIME: Fall, when blooms fade. Dig very deep to get all roots.

PROPAGATION: Seed.

DON'T PICK.

RANGE: Many parts of the United States and Mexico.

LIZARD-TAIL (*Saururus cernuus*). Lizard-tail Family

Interestingly veined heart-shaped leaves. The deeply scented white flower spike arches over in a curve at the top suggesting the appearance of a lizard's tail (In Latin *sauros* means lizard). This is a "feeling" plant, its blooms soft and feathery to touch.

COLOR: White.

HEIGHT: 2 to 5 feet.

SEASON OF BLOOM: Summer.

LOCATION: Along streams, edge of ponds, in boggy, wet meadows and marshes.

SOIL: Sandy loam.

TRANSPLANTING TIME: Early spring or fall.

PROPAGATION: Division.

FRAGRANT.

MAY PICK. Makes charming summer bouquets.

RANGE: Maine to Florida and westward to Ontario and Texas.

MAY-APPLE, WILD MANDRAKE
(*Podophyllum peltatum*). Barberry Family

Grows in lush green colonies of a hundred or more. Like a queen beneath her canopy, the snowy yellow-centered blossom stands erect, or gracefully nodding, in regal dignity. For this is the flower that swings beneath a pair of shiny, many-pointed parasol-like leaves. Edible berries, lemon-shaped, called May-apples, follow. These make good marmalade and jelly; also a popular Southern drink composed of May-apple juice, wine and sugar. But never forget that the *leaves* and *roots* are poisonous, or that the berries must be fully ripe and yellow to be eaten.

COLOR: White.

HEIGHT: 12 to 18 inches.

SEASON OF BLOOM: Spring and early summer.

LOCATION: Wet meadows, woodlands, shaded areas, along moist banks.

SOIL: Acid to neutral.

TRANSPLANTING TIME: Spring.

PROPAGATION: Division.

DON'T PICK.

RANGE: Quebec to Texas.

OXEYE-DAISY, COMMON
WHITE DAISY (*Chrysanthemum
leucanthemum*). Daisy Family
One of summer's loveliest wildflower
bouquets is composed of Daisies. They
last many days in water. The Daisy is a
subject of poem and song; a favorite
with children and artists; the ingredient
of daisy chains; and a way to see if "he
loves you." In Europe and China the
tender young shoots are relished in
salads.

COLOR: White.
HEIGHT: 15 to 24 inches.
SEASON OF BLOOM: Summer.
LOCATION: Open fields and sunny
meadows.
SOIL: Adaptable.
TRANSPLANTING TIME: Spring or
fall.
PROPAGATION: Division of clumps
in early spring.
DO PICK.
RANGE: Naturalized from Europe
across the United States and Canada.

PIPSISSEWA, PRINCE'S PINE
(*Chimaphila umbellata*). Shinleaf
Family
On hillsides among pines, rhododen-
drons and spreading laurel you discover
the solitary stalks of this charming
wildling. Each stem pushes up through
a thick mat of brown woodland floor.
Narrow leaves, dark green and toothed,
bear a distinctive, almost white midriff.
On each single upright stem terminal
clusters of tiny nodding flowers give off

a subtle forest fragrance. The blooms
are in the form of an umbel or "little
umbrella," hence the Latin *umbellata*.
Actually, this little treasure is a shrub.

COLOR: Creamy white or pale
pink, with a central fringe of gold
stamens.
HEIGHT: 4 to 7 inches.
SEASON OF BLOOM: Late June.
LOCATION: In dry woodlands,
often near pines, in filtered shade.
SOIL: Acid. Prefers rich but sandy
woodsy soil; coniferous tree refuse.
TRANSPLANTING TIME: Spring or
fall.
PROPAGATION: Seed or careful
removal of runners.
FRAGRANT.
DON'T PICK.
RANGE: Eastern United States
and Canada; closely related species in
California.

RATTLESNAKE PLANTAIN
(*Epipactis tesselata*). Orchid Family
Enchanting patterns of pale-green pen-
ciling mark the gray-green leaves. At the
center of a rosette of leaves tiny green-
white flowers open all the way up a
slender stalk. The plant transplants well
and easily and will flourish all winter in
a terrarium, where it combines delight-
fully with a few red Partridge Berry
stems.

COLOR: Greenish white.
HEIGHT: 5 to 8 inches.
SEASON OF BLOOM: July to Sep-
tember.

LOCATION: In shady areas, under hemlock, pine and spruce trees, along the north side of stone walls.
SOIL: Acid, cool.
TRANSPLANTING TIME: Early fall.
PROPAGATION: Division.
DON'T PICK.
RANGE: Eastern Canada, Northeastern and North Central states.

THIMBLEWEED, TALL ANEMONE (*Anemone virginiana*). Buttercup Family

Compound leaves in opposite pairs up the main stalk are deep, dark green and slightly hairy, also conspicuously veined, each with many points. Flowers, one inch or less across, are not particularly noticeable. Seedpods are the shape and size of a good-sized thimble, hence the name. Honeybees, drawn by the nectar, along with bumblebees, fertilize the plant. Try drying the seed cases for indoor winter arrangements. Some dye these as well.
COLOR: Greenish white.
HEIGHT: 2 to 3 feet.

SEASON OF BLOOM: Summer.
LOCATION: High woodlands, thickets, banks, shaded meadows, along stone walls and roadsides.
SOIL: Acid to neutral. Moist.
TRANSPLANTING TIME: Early spring or, fall.
PROPAGATION: Seed; division of crowns.
DON'T PICK.
RANGE: Nova Scotia to South Carolina and west to Kansas.

ROUND-LEAVED SUNDEW (*Drosera rotundifolia*). Sundew Family

Here is a ferocious plant with a carnivorous nature. Hairy and sticky leaves one and one-half inches wide, glistening with sticky "dew," lure insects, curl around the ensnared and luckless prey, and the plant promptly proceeds to digest them. The exotic sap is deep purple. Small star-shaped flowers that open only in sunshine are innocent and appealing. Each has five petals. The blossoms open in succession up a slender red stem.
COLOR: White.
HEIGHT: 4 to 9 inches.
SEASON OF BLOOM: Summer.
LOCATION: Wet meadows, low woodlands, boggy areas.
SOIL: Quite acid. Needs an established growth of sphagnum moss.
TRANSPLANTING TIME: Spring.
PROPAGATION: Seed; division.
DON'T PICK.
RANGE: Northern states and Canada.

SWEET-SCENTED BEDSTRAW
(*Galium triflorum*). Madder Family
Romantic olden-time customs are associated with the sweet-scented foliage. It
is said to have lined the Christ Child's
manger. It was also a strewing herb of
the Middle Ages. Country folk used the
dried foliage to stuff mattresses.

COLOR: White.
HEIGHT: 1 to 3 feet.
SEASON OF BLOOM: Summer.
LOCATION: High and low fields
and woodlands, in full sun or partial
shade.
SOIL: Adaptable.
TRANSPLANTING TIME: Spring.
PROPAGATION: Seed.
FRAGRANT. Foliage smells like
vanilla, especially when dried.
MAY PICK.
RANGE: Across the Northern and
Midwestern states.

TALL MEADOW-RUE (*Thalictrum
polygamum*). Buttercup Family
Blue-green lusterless foliage resembles
that of Columbine. It is delicate and
sways in the slightest breeze. Small
blossoms with conspicuous threadlike
stamens appear in clusters, each one
starry, feathery and as ethereal as
thistledown or a snowflake. For beauty
and detail study the flower with a magnifier. Host to many bees and a great
variety of moths and butterflies, all of
which fertilize it.

COLOR: White.
HEIGHT: 3 to 6 feet.
SEASON OF BLOOM: July to Sep-
tember.
LOCATION: Marshes, open
swamps, low damp meadows
SOIL: Moist.
TRANSPLANTING TIME: Early
spring or fall.
PROPAGATION: Seed; division.
FRAGRANT. Sweet meadow scent.
MAY PICK.
RANGE: Southern Canada to Ohio
and southward in cool areas.

VIRGIN'S-BOWER, TRAVELER'S
JOY, CLEMATIS *(Clematis virginiana)*. Buttercup Family
Masses of vine and blossoms tumble
over bushes and stone walls. Often
climbs shrubs and low trees, clinging by
a twist of a leaf stem. In autumn
clusters of silvery-green and feathery
awns give rise to the popular name
"Old Man's Beard." When magnified
these are like tiny twisted tails. The
appealing flowers are a foam of white,
light and airy as thistledown. Coarse
leaves, patterned and jagged-edged, develop in threesomes.

COLOR: White.
HEIGHT: Climbing to 15 feet.
SEASON OF BLOOM: Summer.
LOCATION: Sunny meadows and
wet fields, in copses by moist roadsides,
along river banks.
SOIL: Alkaline to neutral. When
planting, add a half cup of ground
lime per plant. Keep roots and base of
plant shaded. Let it climb into sunlight.
Must have something to cling to.
TRANSPLANTING TIME: Spring.
PROPAGATION: Seed; cuttings;
layering.
FRAGRANT. Like new-mown hay in
sunlight.
MAY PICK.
RANGE: Nova Scotia to Georgia
and west to Kansas.

WASHINGTON LILY, SHASTA
LILY *(Lilium washingtonianum)*. Lily
Family
Dramatic and glorious lily found in the
Sierras, also in the foothills of Yosemite
and the Columbia River areas. Sometimes as many as twenty blossoms open
on a single stalk. Even more white and
glistening than the well-loved cultivated
Easter Lily. At home at an altitude of
three thousand to over seven thousand
feet. Handsome dark-green glossy leaves
appear almost varnished. A breathtaking
sight to come upon is a few stalks of
these beauties of the West. Not rare,
but they seldom grow in masses. In
variety *purpureum* the flowers change to
lilac-purple as they mature.

COLOR: White.
HEIGHT: 2 to 4 feet.
SEASON OF BLOOM: Summer.
LOCATION: In the foothills of the
West, high shaded woodland areas,
moist forest fringes.
SOIL: Acid to neutral.
TRANSPLANTING TIME: Fall.
PROPAGATION: Seed; lifting and
replanting bulbs. Plant the bulb on its
side. Difficult to grow in gardens except
in favored sections of the Pacific
Northwest.
FRAGRANT. Sweet and spicy scent
suggesting a carnation.
MAY PICK.
RANGE: See opening statement in
descriptive paragraph.

WILD CALLA, WATER ARUM

(*Calla palustris*). Arum Family
An appealing swamp flower with a heart-shaped leaf enhanced by swirling, graceful lines and a tapering point. The yellow spadix is covered with diminutive florets. Here is a plant fertilized by pond snails. In midsummer clustered red berries ripen, resembling those of the Jack-in-the-pulpit. At home in cold bogs in the northern parts of the United States. In Europe the starchy root is ground into a meal and used to make bread.

COLOR: Greenish white.
HEIGHT: 5 to 10 inches.
SEASON OF BLOOM: Summer.
LOCATION: Sunny, wet meadows, swamps, bogs, along streams.
SOIL: Rich loam.
TRANSPLANTING TIME: Early spring. Plant in a bog garden or in a few inches of water at the edge of a pond in a sunny place.
PROPAGATION: Seed; division of rhizomes.
DON'T PICK.
RANGE: Maine to Virginia and west to Minnesota.

WATER-HEMLOCK, SPOTTED COWBANE, MUSQUASH ROOT

(*Cicuta maculata*). Carrot Family
White blossoms open in attractive, loose, misty white clusters, branching off from a dull stem. The stalk is streaked and spotted with magenta. Minute florets are especially beautiful when seen through a magnifying lens. Here is a rather common plant closely related to the deadly hemlock that killed Socrates, and was used by the Greeks to extinguish all those they wished to be rid of! It is extremely poisonous to eat; one leaf, one pea-sized bit of the root can cause painful death. Named from the Anglo-Saxon *hemlic*— the general title for poisonous plants.

COLOR: White.
HEIGHT: 3 to 6 feet.
SEASON OF BLOOM: Summer.
LOCATION: Swamps, marshes, damp fields.
SOIL: Acid.
TRANSPLANTING TIME: Too venomous to transplant.
PROPAGATION: Seed, division of tuberous roots.
DON'T PICK.
RANGE: New Brunswick to Florida and west to New Mexico.

WINTERGREEN, CHECKER-BERRY, TEABERRY

(*Gaultheria procumbens*). Heath Family
Nodding vase-shaped flowers appear here and there on the short stems, always in the shade of attractive, firm, glossy oval leaves. Crush a leaf for the pungent and delicious wintergreen flavor. The red berries are sought not only by birds and animals but by children because of that same flavor. Gather and dry the leaves to make your own wintergreen tea: steep in boiling water until the desired strength. You find a similar aromatic taste in Sweet Birch. Curiously, the sap of both these unrelated plants has a high concentration of methyl salicylate—known commercially as aspirin!

COLOR: White or pink-tinged.
HEIGHT: 2 to 5 inches.
SEASON OF BLOOM: Late spring and summer.

LOCATION: High dry woodlands and open places, especially near evergreen trees.
SOIL: Acid.
TRANSPLANTING TIME: Spring or fall.
PROPAGATION: Seed, cuttings, division.
DON'T PICK.
RANGE: Newfoundland south to Georgia and west to Manitoba.

CLIMBING WILD CUCUMBER, WILD BALSAM-APPLE (*Echinocystis lobata*). Gourd Family
Botanical name comes from the Greek for "spiny bladder" and refers to the fruits, which are well armed by sharp spines. These are two inches long, cucumberlike, becoming papery and not really fearsome. Note especially the appealing corkscrew tendrils reaching out for something to cling to and climb about. Beautiful and fast-growing, a luxuriant climber, with leaves that usually have five sharp, angular points. Six-petaled flowers are borne in casual loose clusters, not showy but unusual.
COLOR: Greenish white.
HEIGHT: 15 to 20 feet, climbing.
SEASON OF BLOOM: Summer.
LOCATION: Bogs, along streams, but will grow on an arbor if well watered.
SOIL: Likes a rich soil.
TRANSPLANTING TIME: This is an annual.
PROPAGATION: Seed.
DON'T PICK.
RANGE: New Brunswick west to Idaho and south to Texas.

CULVER'S ROOT (*Veronicastrum virginicum*). Snapdragon Family
The Latin name is a combination of both Veronica and Aster; the plant blends the features of both. Its common name is for a Dr. Culver, who popularized the plant and found the root a useful cathartic. Flowers open all the way up several tapering stalks and often bend at the top, suggesting the tail of a very young kitten. Leaves grow in whorls of four to seven.
COLOR: White.
HEIGHT: 2 to 7 feet.
SEASON OF BLOOM: Summer and early fall.
LOCATION: Moist woodlands, fields, thickets, often along old roads.
SOIL: Moderately acid.
TRANSPLANTING TIME: Spring.
PROPAGATION: Seed.
MAY PICK.
RANGE: Vermont to Texas.

DAISY FLEABANE (*Erigeron ramosus*). Daisy Family
Countless small myriad-petaled yellow-centered daisies are borne on many-branched flower stalks. Almost as soft and delicate as Baby's Breath. Grows everywhere. So common we may over-look its charm and magic. Do pause and appreciate it with a magnifying glass. Gather for enchanting summer indoor bouquets.

COLOR: White.
HEIGHT: 1 to 2 feet.
SEASON OF BLOOM: Summer.
LOCATION: Sunny, dry meadows and fields.
SOIL: Prefers poor, gravelly soil. Adaptable.
TRANSPLANTING TIME: Spring.
PROPAGATION: Seed; also by lifting and separating rooted pieces.

FRAGRANT. Meadow-in-the-sun scent.
MAY PICK.
RANGE: Across the continent from Canada to Southern states.

DATURA, ANGEL'S TRUMPET, THORN APPLE, JIMSON WEED (*Datura stramonium*). Nightshade Family
Naturalized from Asia. Trumpet-shaped flowers, often with five points, open to spread their fragrance far and wide. As delightful as the flowers are, equally so are the appealing fat round seedpods, each with a green frilled ruff around its neck. Dry these and plant them for more Angel's Trumpets. Do not eat any part, as it is all poisonous. The plant furnishes an important drug with narcotic, anodyne and antispasmodic properties, commonly known as stramo-nium.

COLOR: White or lavender.
HEIGHT: 1 to 5 feet.
SEASON OF BLOOM: Summer.
LOCATION: Sunny meadows, fields, waste areas.
SOIL: Rich.
TRANSPLANTING TIME: Spring; but this plant is an annual, so best from seed.
PROPAGATION: Easy from seed.
FRAGRANT.
MAY PICK.
RANGE: Mostly Middle Atlantic, Southern and Lower Central states.

EVENING LYCHNIS, WHITE CAMPION *(Lychnis alba)*. Pink Family

A charming plant whose pointed leaves gracefully curl at the ends. Topping each stalk are appealing white flowers that open in the evening. The deeply cleft petals emerge from an oval vase-shaped cup that is sticky, hairy. The cup is marked with maroon ribs. Touch a bit of magic by wandering through a meadow on a moonlit night where these flowers stand out like stars tossed among the grasses. The name comes from the Greek *lychnos*, meaning lamp. Originally naturalized from Europe, it is found in our Eastern states and in the Rocky Mountains.

    COLOR: White.
    HEIGHT: 1 to 2 feet.
    SEASON OF BLOOM: Summer and fall.
    LOCATION: Sunny meadows.
    SOIL: Adaptable.
    TRANSPLANTING TIME: Spring.
    PROPAGATION: Seed, division.
    FRAGRANT.
    MAY PICK.
    RANGE: Eastern and Central states and in the Rockies.

PEARLY EVERLASTING, MOON-SHINE *(Anaphalis margaritacea)*. Daisy Family

Blossoms with tawny yellow centers and crisp white petal-like bracts. Leaves are sage green, stems white and woolly. Hang the stalks topped by blooms upside down to dry for winter bouquets. One of the most beautiful and showy of the everlasting wildflowers. Heads of tiny flowers are pressed close into a prim rosette. At night an assortment of interesting moths are drawn by the nectar; by day, butterflies.

    COLOR: White.
    HEIGHT: 1 to 3 feet.
    SEASON OF BLOOM: Summer and fall.
    LOCATION: Open dry meadows and country roadsides.
    SOIL: Light, well-drained.
    TRANSPLANTING TIME: Spring or fall.
    PROPAGATION: Seed; lifting and separating pieces of root. Plant in a sunny location.
    MAY PICK.
    RANGE: Eastern and Central United States, and a variant form in the West on up to Alaska.

SOIL: Arid.

TRANSPLANTING TIME: Spring or fall.

PROPAGATION: Seed.

FRAGRANT. Plant and flowers strongly scented.

DO PICK.

RANGE: Throughout many parts of the United States, naturalized from Europe.

RATTLESNAKE ROOT, WHITE LETTUCE (*Prenanthes alba*). Daisy Family

The interesting toothed and cut foliage suggests oakleaf lettuce. Branching stalks of drooping flowers in loose panicles rise above the greenery. Indian lore tells us this plant was once considered effective against rattlesnake bites.

QUEEN ANNE'S LACE, WILD CARROT (*Daucus carota*). Carrot Family

A beautiful lacy head of minuscule florets arranged in a radiating pattern. A delight in summer bouquets. May be dried to enhance winter arrangements. Often called Bird's Nest because it goes to seed like a bunch of tangled wool in a small brown cage. The root resembles the cultivated carrot, hence the name. The edible carrot plant was probably a variant form of this wild plant, discovered in remote times; no one knows. But the Wild Carrot root is not edible. Host to the golden swallowtail butterflies seeking nectar.

COLOR: White.

HEIGHT: 2 to 3 feet.

SEASON OF BLOOM: Summer and fall.

LOCATION: Dry meadows, fields, woodland fringes, waste places.

COLOR: White rays with a purplish involucre.

HEIGHT: 2 to 4 feet.

SEASON OF BLOOM: Summer and fall.

LOCATION: At edge of woodlands.

SOIL: Somewhat acid.

TRANSPLANTING TIME: Spring.

PROPAGATION: Division.

MAY PICK.

RANGE: Maine to Minnesota and south to Georgia and Kentucky.

SLENDER LADIES'-TRESSES
(*Spiranthes gracilis*). Orchid Family
Its botanical name, from the Greek meaning "spiral-flowered," is descriptive of the blossom arrangement. Tiny delicate blossoms twisting up a stalk suggest braids of hair in small scale. A shy, modest flower whose exquisite beauty must be revealed with a magnifier. Cherished for the deeply sweet fragrance suggestive of the blooms of the horse-chestnut. Fertilized by the large bumblebees, also by smaller bees and other insects.

COLOR: Creamy white, sometimes greenish.

HEIGHT: 10 to 22 inches.

SEASON OF BLOOM: Summer, fall.

LOCATION: Sunny fields and fringes of woodlands. Also light shade.

SOIL: Grows best in dryish soil.

TRANSPLANTING TIME: Spring.

PROPAGATION: Seed.

FRAGRANT.

DON'T PICK.

RANGE: Nova Scotia to Florida, Manitoba to Texas.

TURTLEHEAD (*Chelone glabra*).
Snapdragon Family
Flowers resemble the head of a turtle with open mouth. Blooms until late in the fall, defying the first frost or two. The main stalk is smooth, the leaves toothed, short-stemmed and lance-shaped, each three to six inches long.

COLOR: Pinkish white or pink.

HEIGHT: 1 to 2 feet.

SEASON OF BLOOM: Summer and fall.

LOCATION: Swamps, low, wet woodlands and meadows.

SOIL: Should be fairly moist and moderately acid.

TRANSPLANTING TIME: Spring or fall.

PROPAGATION: Seed; cuttings; division. Good for bog gardens and at edge of streams and ponds. Part shade best, with a heavy mulch of rotted manure and leaf mold to feed the surface roots and provide dampness.

DON'T PICK.

RANGE: Nova Scotia south to Georgia and west to Minnesota.

Season of bloom: Summer and fall.
Location: Still waters of shallow lakes, ponds, river margins.
Soil: Mucky rich black earth.
Transplanting time: Spring.
Propagation: Seed; division of clumps of rhizomes weighed down by rocks until rooted.
Fragrant.
Don't pick.
Range: Newfoundland to Florida, and Michigan to Texas.

WHITE THOROUGHWORT
(*Eupatorium album*). Daisy Family
Very small downy flowers in clustered heads crown each leaf stalk. Plant rough and hairy—similar to the popular cultivated perennial Ageratum. The botanical name honors Mithridates Eupator, King of Pontus, a land adjacent to the Black Sea. The ancients believed that the plant, when applied locally, helped heal broken bones.
Color: White.
Height: 1 to 3 feet.
Season of bloom: Summer.
Location: Woodlands, fringe of shade, pine barrens.
Soil: Sandy.
Transplanting time: Spring or fall.
Propagation: Division of clumps.
May pick.
Range: New York to Florida and Louisiana.

WHITE WATER LILY (*Nymphaea odorata*). Water Lily Family
Snowy white flowers with golden stamens at the centers are three to five inches across. They float amidst glossy flat leaves on the still waters of remote ponds. Named *Nymphaea* for the mythological nymphs of ancient Greece who lived in ponds and secluded lakes. Young unopened leaves are said to enhance the flavor of soups and stews.
Color: White.
Height: Floating leaves; flowers held above the water.

WILD MINT (*Mentha arvensis*).
Mint Family
One of the very few American mints. Furry small blossoms clustering around the main stem half-hide themselves at the base of each pair of sharply toothed leaves. A handful of these leaves steeped in boiling water for five minutes

makes a pot of mint tea—delicious hot or cold, with honey. A few sprigs enhance all fruit drinks. Especially good with pineapple juice. And, of course, there is the mint julep.

COLOR: White or pale lavender.
HEIGHT: 1 to 2 feet.
SEASON OF BLOOM: Summer and fall.
LOCATION: Wet and dry areas in sun or shade.
SOIL: Neutral.
TRANSPLANTING TIME: Spring or summer.
PROPAGATION: By runners; spreads fast.
MAY PICK.
RANGE: Newfoundland and southern Canada to Georgia and west to Nebraska; also in far West.

MICHAELMAS DAISY, HEATH ASTER (*Aster ericoides*). Daisy Family Blooms until late fall, even beyond the first frost or two. Undaunted by chilly weather and cold nights. Common in New York, New Jersey and Pennsylvania, where each plant opens hundreds of tiny daisylike blossoms with yellow disc centers along the roadsides. Especially favored by honeybees. In areas where it grows, your wildflower honey will surely have nectar from this flower.

COLOR: White.

HEIGHT: 1 to 3 feet.
SEASON OF BLOOM: Fall.
LOCATION: Along dry roadsides, in meadows.
SOIL: Neutral.
TRANSPLANTING TIME: Spring or fall.
PROPAGATION: Separation of rooted shoots.
MAY PICK.
RANGE: Maine to Minnesota and to Florida and Missouri.

SHARP-LEAF WOOD ASTER (*Aster acuminatus*). Daisy Family Coarse-toothed deep-green foliage is often arranged in a circle below the long-stemmed fragrant flowers. Blossoms casual and windblown. An old-time Greek legend tells us that the Aster was fashioned out of stardust one time when Virgo, gazing down from the black night above to a warring earth, sadly wept.

COLOR: Lilac-white.
HEIGHT: 10 to 16 inches.
SEASON OF BLOOM: Fall.
LOCATION: High, dry woodlands, thickets, meadows, along roadsides.
SOIL: Acid.
TRANSPLANTING TIME: Spring.
PROPAGATION: Division.
FRAGRANT.
MAY PICK.
RANGE: Labrador to Georgia.

BIRD'S-FOOT VIOLET (*Viola pedata*). Violet Family
State flower of Wisconsin, where it grows by the acre. Flourishes in New England, especially Massachusetts, but can be found as far south as Florida. Out of feathery, fernlike leaves emerge numerous light-lilac blooms, each with a touch of yellow or orange at the center. A wildflower that transplants readily to your own land. According to the old Greek legend, Zeus created the Violet as a particularly fragrant food for Io, the daughter of Inachus, the river god. *Io* is the Greek word for Violet.

COLOR: Light violet.
HEIGHT: 4 to 10 inches.
SEASON OF BLOOM: Spring.
LOCATION: Dry sandy fields, open woods.
SOIL: Acid, sandy, with rotted oak leaves, pine or hemlock needles.
TRANSPLANTING TIME: Spring.
PROPAGATION: Seed, division of clumpy plants in early fall.
FRAGRANT.
DON'T PICK.
RANGE: Massachusetts west to Minnesota and south to Florida.

COMMON VIOLET (*Viola cucullata*). Violet Family
Napoleon liked to have a small bunch of Violets (various species) on his desk in their season. Try candying the deep-purple blooms for an afternoon tea treat. Lovely to eat, to wear, to admire as you walk by. A part of springtime is to sit on some comfortable bank and pick bouquets of Violets for families, friends and yourself. Spreads rapidly and grows just about anywhere. Easy to transplant.

COLOR: Rich purple.
HEIGHT: 3 to 7 inches.
SEASON OF BLOOM: Spring, sometimes again in fall.
LOCATION: Widely distributed, especially in moist meadows, along streams, in woodlands.
SOIL: Adaptable, but grows best in loamy soil in a cool location. Suffers if not well watered in dry weather.
TRANSPLANTING TIME: Spring or fall.
PROPAGATION: Seed; division of roots.
MAY PICK.
RANGE: Quebec to Georgia.

CRESTED DWARF IRIS (*Iris cristata*). Iris Family
Iris was the "rainbow flower" to the

Orientals and also to the ancient Greeks. This dwarf species flourishes in great sweeps in the mountains of North Carolina and Oklahoma. Also on hillsides and along streams. Easy to move and multiplies readily. A dainty, delicate and favorite spring flower. The charming tapering lance-shaped foliage is among the earliest signs of spring. How welcome it is after a long, cold winter—something green and full of promise.

COLOR: Lavender-blue, the sepals with a yellow crest.

HEIGHT: 3 to 4 inches.

SEASON OF BLOOM: Spring.

LOCATION: Thickets and woodlands, along streams.

SOIL: Sandy loam, sun and part shade.

TRANSPLANTING TIME: Summer.

PROPAGATION: Seed; division in summer.

MAY PICK.

RANGE: Maryland to Georgia and west to Oklahoma.

PROPAGATION: Seed. Self-sows freely.

MAY PICK.

RANGE: Alaska and most of Canada, south to North Carolina and west to California.

FORGET-ME-NOT (Myosotis scorpioides). Borage Family

State flower of Alaska. Originally from Europe and Asia, but now naturalized in many parts of America. May be discovered on high mountainsides in Montana, where it is subtly fragrant with a wisteria-like scent. Enchanting tiny blue blooms, often touched with pink, appear on a plant composed of sprawling, fine-hairy stems. Lasts well indoors in vases. Especially charming in miniature bouquets. A longtime symbol of loving remembrance, friendship and loyalty.

COLOR: Light blue.

HEIGHT: 6 to 15 inches.

SEASON OF BLOOM: Spring, summer and fall.

LOCATION: Sunny fields, damp meadows and marshes, along streams.

SOIL: Prefers boggy soil. Will flourish almost in water—also in a drier flower border, but less luxuriantly.

TRANSPLANTING TIME: Spring. Easy.

HEPATICA, LIVERLEAF (Hepatica triloba). Buttercup Family

Appealing tiny flowers of this woodland favorite are the true heralds of spring. Furry-stemmed blossoms in lilac, pink, blue or white appear before the new three-lobed leaves, which are very hairy. Blooms have white filaments and anthers. May be found early, early among the wet leaves and rocks on a protected woodland slope. Must be sought to be discovered.

COLOR: Lilac, blue, white, pink.

HEIGHT: 3 to 5 inches.

SEASON OF BLOOM: Early spring.

LOCATION: Under trees, on rocky wooded slopes and trails.

SOIL: Slightly acid to neutral.

TRANSPLANTING TIME: Fall.

PROPAGATION: Seed; division.

DON'T PICK.

RANGE: Nova Scotia to Manitoba and south to Florida.

PASQUEFLOWER *(Anemone patens)*. Buttercup Family
State flower of South Dakota. Among the earliest to bloom, even while snow remains, and often around Easter time, hence the name. The flower lies snug in a covering of silky fur that keeps it warm in chill winds. Stems and blossom exterior both downy and soft to touch. The delicate violet-blue seems to have caught its tone from the magic of a spring sky. *Anemos* is the Greek word for wind; the botanical name *Anemone* alludes to the high mountainside habitat of many species of these ethereal flowers. The fruiting head, resembling that of the Clematis, is a tossing windblown tangle of long feathery tails as charming as the flower.

JACK-IN-THE-PULPIT, INDIAN TURNIP *(Arisaema triphyllum)*. Arum Family
Beneath an umbrella of one or two three-parted leaves stands the single stem of this beloved and familiar woodland plant. Observe the wonderfully sinuous curving way the beginning shoots emerge from the wet spring earth, the vivid stripes and markings of the mature plant already visible. A striped hood gradually unfolds to arch over an erect stalk where the actual tiny blooms form. A great cluster of dazzling red berries appears in late summer. The Indians used to eat the root boiled, hence the alternate name, Indian Turnip. Turns pale green in light woods, deep purple in dim, shadowed glades.

    COLOR: Purple, brown, green.
    HEIGHT: 1 to 3 feet.
    SEASON OF BLOOM: Late spring.
    LOCATION: Woodlands, thickets, other semi-shaded areas.
    SOIL: Acid.
    TRANSPLANTING TIME: Spring.
    PROPAGATION: Seed; division.
    DON'T PICK.
    RANGE: Eastern North America and west to Kansas.

    COLOR: Pale violet.
    HEIGHT: 6 to 14 inches.
    SEASON OF BLOOM: Early spring.
    LOCATION: In the West, on prairies and high pastures, along mountain slopes.
    SOIL: Well-drained limy loam.
    TRANSPLANTING TIME: Early spring or fall.
    PROPAGATION: Seed; division of crowns; root cuttings.
    DON'T PICK.
    RANGE: Illinois northward and westward to Colorado, Montana, British Columbia and Alaska.

VIRGINIA COWSLIP, VIRGINIA BLUEBELLS (*Mertensia virginica*). Borage Family
Delicate china-blue bell-shaped flowers that start out as pink buds swing from nodding stalks. Fleshy blue-green foliage appears ahead of the blossoms. Grows along southern stream banks, in rich bottom land. Spreads rampantly when conditions are right. Transplants readily and self-sows.

SKUNK CABBAGE (*Symplocarpus foetidus*). Arum Family
Plant appears at spring's beginning, unfurling a curving rhythmic flower sheath rather like a shell. This shell, while beautiful to look at, is sinister, for it lures insects inside and to their death. All the same, the swirling pattern of these first shapes is irresistible. The later cabbagelike leaves are up to three feet long and one foot wide, and they make a magnificent groundcover. Foliage gives out an unpleasant mustard-plasterlike odor, but only when crushed. In their juvenile state the leaves are quite edible if boiled in several waters; a spoonful of baking soda in the cooking frees them from their strong scent. An old-time remedy for rheumatism.
COLOR: Dark purple, red, green.
HEIGHT: Flowers, 1 foot; leaves, 2 feet.
SEASON OF BLOOM: Spring.
LOCATION: Low, wet woodlands and bogs, along shady edge of streams.
SOIL: Acid to neutral.
TRANSPLANTING TIME: Fall.
PROPAGATION: Division of clumps.
MAY PICK.
RANGE: Southern Canada to Florida and Louisiana.

COLOR: Buds pink, flowers pale blue.
HEIGHT: 1 to 2 feet.
SEASON OF BLOOM: Spring.
LOCATION: Along streams, in low woodlands and meadows.
SOIL: Adaptable, but best in rich humus, acid to neutral.
TRANSPLANTING TIME: Spring. Plant under deciduous trees, at edge of shrubbery, on shaded side of rock garden.
PROPAGATION: Seed, sown when ripe.
DON'T PICK.
RANGE: New York to Missouri and Tennessee.

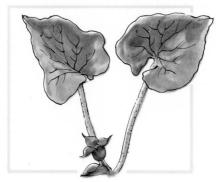

WILD GINGER, INDIAN GINGER, MONKEY JUGS (*Asarum canadense*). Birthwort Family

Slightly ruffled woolly heart-shaped leaves on hairy stems partly conceal the intriguing small brownish-purple blossoms. Flowers appear deep down in the heart of the plant at ground level, each calyx having three pointed, petal-like divisions. When open it resembles a miniature brown jug. Is inconspicuous and almost the color of the matted brown forest leaves that background it and sometimes nearly hide it. The rootstalk sends out an aroma of ginger, hence the name. This rootstalk can be boiled, cut up and used to make candied ginger or to flavor cakes, cookies and puddings.

COLOR: Brown-purple.
HEIGHT: 6 to 12 inches.
SEASON OF BLOOM: Early spring.
LOCATION: High shady woods.
SOIL: Acid. Prefers fairly rich soil.
TRANSPLANTING TIME: Spring or fall.
PROPAGATION: Division. Good edging plants in a shady border or shaded area in rock garden.
DON'T PICK.
RANGE: New Hampshire to·North Carolina and west to Kansas. A rather similar species grows in the far West.

BLUETS, QUAKER-LADIES, INNOCENCE (*Houstonia caerulea*). Madder Family

The Latin name is for Dr. William Houston, an eighteenth-century Scottish botanical writer. From the midst of a fine tangle of narrow foliage and stems emerge prim, neat little sky-blue blossoms with white centers stained gold. Crisp and clean as enamel. Usually grow in a large colony. Watch them sway stiffly as a slight zephyr riffles over. Fertilized by bees and the clouded sulphur Butterfly.

COLOR: Blue.
HEIGHT: 3 to 6 inches.
SEASON OF BLOOM: Late spring.
LOCATION: In open fields and rocky, sunny meadows.
SOIL: Acid, light and rich.
TRANSPLANTING TIME: Spring or fall.
PROPAGATION: Seed; division in September. This species self-sows. Soil should be kept moist.
MAY PICK.
RANGE: Nova Scotia to Georgia and Missouri.

BLUE-EYED GRASS (*Sisyrinchium angustifolium*). Iris Family

Deep violet-blue flowers like small stars scatter through the grassy foliage of this stiff little plant. Note the sharp-pointed petals that prick if you don't watch out. Also, observe the blossom with a magnifier to better appreciate the beautifully marked center with a six-pointed star accented with bright golden-yellow. It was one of Thoreau's favorite flowers.

COLOR: Deep violet-blue.
HEIGHT: 6 to 13 inches.
SEASON OF BLOOM: Spring and summer.
LOCATION: Fields, wet meadows, sunny hillsides.
SOIL: Prefers compost of peat and loam.
TRANSPLANTING TIME: Spring or fall.
PROPAGATION: Division.
DON'T PICK.
RANGE: Newfoundland to British Columbia and south to Virginia and the Rockies.

JACOB'S-LADDER (*Polemonium vanbruntiae*). Phlox Family
Violet bell-shaped flowers nod in bud, straighten as they open. The Latin name is in honor of the early Greek philosopher Polemon. Note the unusual leaf formation suggestive of a ladder, hence the common name. This alludes to Jacob and his dream of angels ascending a ladder into heaven. Somewhat rare except in the Northern states.

COLOR: Violet.
HEIGHT: 10 to 24 inches.
SEASON OF BLOOM: Spring and summer.
LOCATION: Marshy fields, stream banks, edge of woods.

SOIL: Thrives in ordinary soil.
TRANSPLANTING TIME: Spring or fall.
PROPAGATION: Seed; division.
DON'T PICK.
RANGE: Vermont to Maryland. Related species in North Central states and Northwest, including British Columbia.

LARGE BLUE FLAG (*Iris versicolor*). Iris Family
Flat lance-shaped leaves emerging from wet meadows and pastures are as appealing as the flowers. The neatly furled deep-blue buds open into violet-blue blossoms, charmingly veined. The pattern of another kind of Iris was copied in designing the French banner in the thirteenth-century wars. Subsequently this stylized fleur-de-lis was employed in many European tapestries, carvings and decorations.

COLOR: Violet-blue or purplish; sometimes slate blue.
HEIGHT: 16 to 30 inches.
SEASON OF BLOOM: Late spring and summer.
LOCATION: Marshes, wet pastures, banks of ponds and streams.
SOIL: Average garden soil, kept moist.
TRANSPLANTING TIME: Spring.
PROPAGATION: Division of clumps.
MAY PICK.
RANGE: Eastern Canada to Pennsylvania and west to Michigan. Rather similar species occur in the Midwest and South Central states.

LEATHERLEAF CLEMATIS
(*Clematis ochroleuca*). Buttercup
Family
Watch for the shaggy yellow-brown
seedpod that is as delightful as the
nodding lavender flowers. Hairy silky
stems, leatherlike foliage, firm to touch.
Each flower stalk rises from the main
stem in the joint where pairs of opposite
leaves have formed. Unlike most
Clematis, this one is not a vine but an
erect herb.
  COLOR: Pale lavender.
  HEIGHT: 1 to 2 feet.
  SEASON OF BLOOM: Spring and
summer.
  LOCATION: Part shade in high
woodlands, meadows.
  SOIL: Adaptable, but sandy loam
with some lime best.
  TRANSPLANTING TIME: Spring or
fall.
  PROPAGATION: Seed; division of
clumps; cuttings.
  DON'T PICK.
  RANGE: New York to Georgia.

ROBIN'S-PLANTAIN (*Erigeron
pulchellus*). Daisy Family
Usually grows in massed groups flour-
ishing in waste areas and sun-baked
places. Lilac-colored ray flowers soft as
feathers and a golden disc center. The
rays are more numerous and narrower
than those of Daisies and Asters, and
also shorter in proportion to the disc.

Foliage is soft and downy. *Pulchellus*,
from the Latin, meaning "beautiful,"
aptly describes these spring and summer
beauties.
  COLOR: Lilac.
  HEIGHT: 10 to 22 inches.
  SEASON OF BLOOM: Spring and
summer.
  LOCATION: Sunny fields, dry
gravelly areas, thickets.
  SOIL: Sandy loam.
  TRANSPLANTING TIME: Summer or
fall. Take the offsets, for the parent
plant usually dies after forming seed.
  PROPAGATION: Offsets.
  MAY PICK.
  RANGE: Nova Scotia to Louisiana.

SEGO LILY, MARIPOSA TULIP
(*Calochortus nuttallii*). Lily Family
State flower of Utah. Greatly revered
there by the inhabitants because the
bulb, when cooked, nourished the
Mormons on their long trek west.
Found all through the Grand Canyon
area, along Bright Angel Trail and
much of the rest of the Southwest.
Flower petals are fluted and slightly
ruffled. Named from the Spanish word
for butterfly, *mariposa*, because of the
gay, vivid markings.
  COLOR: White, penciled or
flushed lilac, a dark spot at the base.
Also a clear pink form.
  HEIGHT: 12 inches.
  SEASON OF BLOOM: Spring and
summer.

LOCATION: Hot, dry regions of the Southwest.

SOIL: Well-drained, sandy, with some leaf mold.

TRANSPLANTING TIME: Dig bulbs when leaves have ripened, store in a box, plant in late October.

PROPAGATION: Seed; offsets. Needs plenty of sunshine, perfect drainage.

MAY PICK.

RANGE: California to Nebraska and South Dakota, and to Arizona and New Mexico.

SELF-HEAL, HEAL-ALL (*Prunella vulgaris*). Mint Family

Here is a country-wide flower found everywhere in America. Adapts itself to and thrives in any soil. Old-time country people used to make brews from the foliage for healing a number of ills, including tonsillitis and any ailments of the jaw or mouth. Constantly visited by bumblebees and small colorful butterflies. An attractive if unassuming groundcover in shade.

COLOR: Purple.

HEIGHT: 6 to 13 inches.

SEASON OF BLOOM: Spring and summer.

LOCATION: In fields and woods, common everywhere.

SOIL: Adaptable, but light soil and some shade best.

TRANSPLANTING TIME: Spring or fall.

PROPAGATION: Division.

MAY PICK.

RANGE: Across Canada and the United States.

SPIDERWORT (*Tradescantia virginiana*). Dayflower Family

Named in honor of John Tradescant, a favorite royal gardener of King Charles I, who brought many exotic plants to England, including this one. Each flower lasts but a day. However, countless fresh ones unfold every morning. The filaments of the six stamens, clothed with long hairs, suggest the spider. Strangely, too, from the jointed stems a mucilaginous thread can be pulled out as fine as a spider web, and it quickly hardens with exposure to air. Stems and leaves make a fine potherb. Each attractive flower has three deep-ultramarine petals.

COLOR: Ultramarine blue.

HEIGHT: 1 to 3 feet.

SEASON OF BLOOM: Spring and summer.

LOCATION: In woods, thickets, everywhere.

SOIL: Should be fertile and fairly moist.

TRANSPLANTING TIME: Spring or early fall.

PROPAGATION: Division.

DO PICK.

RANGE: Northeast, west to South Dakota and Arkansas.

WILD BLUE PHLOX (*Phlox divaricata*). Phlox Family
Florets gather in loose clusters topping single stalks. Flourishes in moist thin woodlands where sunlight filters through the high branches above. Stems somewhat sticky, fine-hairy. Leaves slim and tapering. The name Phlox comes from the Greek, meaning flame, and refers to the brilliant tints of many species and varieties.

COLOR: Lavender.
HEIGHT: 9 to 18 inches.
SEASON OF BLOOM: May to early June.
LOCATION: Open woods.
SOIL: Acid to neutral.
TRANSPLANTING TIME: Spring or fall.
PROPAGATION: Seed; cuttings; division of roots. Spreads rapidly when established.
FRAGRANT.
DO PICK.
RANGE: Quebec to Florida and Texas.

WILD GERANIUM, CRANESBILL (*Geranium maculatum*). Geranium Family
Deeply indented five-lobed leaves are soft to touch and somewhat downy. Occasionally the ten anthers are a delicate peacock blue. The dainty flowers appear in shadowy areas along country lanes and in woodlands everywhere. One of its names, Cranesbill, is suggested by the seedpod, which has a long slim beak like that of a crane. A decoction from boiled cut-up roots was an old-time remedy for sore throats.

COLOR: Rose-lavender.
HEIGHT: 1 to 2 feet.
SEASON OF BLOOM: Spring and summer.
LOCATION: Low, moist woodlands and fields.
SOIL: Acid to neutral.
TRANSPLANTING TIME: Spring or fall.
PROPAGATION: Seed; division.
DON'T PICK.
RANGE: Across southern Canada and eastern half of the United States to North Carolina and west to Arkansas.

AMERICAN BROOKLIME, SPEEDWELL (*Veronica americana*). Snapdragon Family
Along streams and in damp woods these tiny vivid blue flowers with white centers cluster loosely at the stem tips. They also develop in the joints between leaf and stem. Oval light-green leaves

are slightly toothed. Its botanical name is in honor of St. Veronica. Discover the piquant flavor by using these flowers and their foliage in early-summer salads.

COLOR: Brilliant blue.
HEIGHT: 6 to 15 inches.
SEASON OF BLOOM: Summer.
LOCATION: By brooks, in ditches, woodlands, swamps.
SOIL: Adaptable.
TRANSPLANTING TIME: Spring or early fall.
PROPAGATION: Division, cuttings.
PICK ONLY IF PLENTY.
RANGE: Widely scattered over North America.

CREEPING BELLFLOWER
(*Campanula rapunculoides*). Bellflower Family
Naturalized from Europe and occasionally escaped from perennial borders here to grow wild. Nodding bell-like flowers open all the way up the single stem beginning at the bottom. Foliage

hairy and soft, scallop-toothed. Beloved by the large furry bumblebees.

COLOR: Purple.
HEIGHT: 2 to 4 feet.
SEASON OF BLOOM: Summer.
LOCATION: In fields and pastures, along fences, roadsides, edge of woods.
SOIL: Neutral, loam or clay.
TRANSPLANTING TIME: Spring or fall.
PROPAGATION: Seed and underground runners.
DO PICK.
RANGE: Northeastern states and southern Canada.

BLUNT-LEAVED MILKWEED
(*Asclepias amplexicaulis*). Milkweed Family
From the center of a pair of ruffled wavy leaves rises a single stalk topped with clusters of tiny lilac florets. The seedpods are long and slim, their shape vaguely suggestive of a heron, especially if your imagination is active. They split open and release hundreds of silky seed tufts.

COLOR: Lilac.
HEIGHT: 2 to 3 feet.
SEASON OF BLOOM: Summer.
LOCATION: Dry meadows and fields, along roadsides, pine barrens.
SOIL: Dry, sandy.
TRANSPLANTING TIME: Spring.
PROPAGATION: Seed.
DON'T PICK.
RANGE: North Carolina to Florida and Texas.

COMMON MILKWEED, SILK-
WEED (*Asclepias syriaca*). Milkweed
Family
One of the most fragrant of wildflowers.
The rich deep scent fills the area where
it grows. Clusters of tiny lavender
florets emerge on a single stalk from the
leaf and stem joints. As appealing as
the flowers are the silky parachutes
released in autumn from a neatly
packed pod. Each one carries a single
seed to a new home. Are these parachutes or ballet dancers? No matter:
they glisten in the sun and are beautiful. Cook the very young shoots, butter
them and eat like asparagus.
    COLOR: Lilac.
    HEIGHT: 3 to 5 feet.
    SEASON OF BLOOM: Summer.
    LOCATION: Roadsides, fields,
waste places—widespread.
    SOIL: Adaptable.
    TRANSPLANTING TIME: Fall.
    PROPAGATION: Seed and root
cuttings; but a very invasive weed.
    FRAGRANT.
    DO PICK.
    RANGE: New Brunswick to North
Carolina and west to Kansas.

FALSE DRAGONHEAD, LION'S-
HEART (*Physostegia virginiana*).
Mint Family
Flaring funnel-shaped blossoms with the
upper lip a little hooded are gathered
at the top of the stems. Also called

Obedient Plant because if individual
flowers are moved sideways they remain
where placed. The stemless lance-
shaped leaves are mostly toothed.
    COLOR: Lilac.
    HEIGHT: 1 to 4 feet.
    SEASON OF BLOOM: Summer.
    LOCATION: Moist meadows, fields,
bogs, along brooksides.
    SOIL: Does well in ordinary soil.
    TRANSPLANTING TIME: Spring or
fall.
    PROPAGATION: Division.
    MAY PICK.
    RANGE: Quebec to Florida and
Texas.

HEARTLEAF TWAYBLADE
(*Listera cordata*). Orchid Family
About halfway up the stem are two
horizontal, stemless and opposite leaves.

At the top of the stem, a spike of scattered, tiny purplish to yellow-green flowers. Twayblade is an old English word meaning "two leaves" (blades). An insect visitor causes the flower to eject a sticky fluid that collects pollen and then clings to the invader and is carried off.

COLOR: Dull purple to yellow-green.
HEIGHT: 5 to 10 inches.
SEASON OF BLOOM: Summer.
LOCATION: Mossy woods, in mountains in South.
SOIL: Acid.
TRANSPLANTING TIME: Spring.
PROPAGATION: Root division.
DON'T PICK.
RANGE: Newfoundland west to Alaska, Colorado, California; south to North Carolina.

LARGE PURPLE FRINGED ORCHIS (*Habenaria fimbriata*). Orchid Family

Host to countless bees and butterflies. Mingles its scent with that of the sunny damp meadows where it grows. Each lobe of the three-parted lip is delicately fringed. As many as twenty flowers may be loosely arranged in a broad spike at the summit of the stem. They commence opening from the bottom.

COLOR: Purple.
HEIGHT: 12 to 30 inches.
SEASON OF BLOOM: Summer.

LOCATION: Meadows, swamps, wet deciduous woods.
SOIL: Acid, moist, boggy.
TRANSPLANTING TIME: September.
PROPAGATION: Division of roots.
FRAGRANT.
DON'T PICK.
RANGE: Newfoundland to Minnesota, south to North Carolina and Tennessee.

DWARF LARKSPUR (*Delphinium tricorne*). Buttercup Family

The name is from the Greek word for dolphin. Note the special charm of each dolphin-shaped bud. The flower opens white, lavender or a deep sky-blue. The blossoms each have a spur and a prominent stalk, giving the whole raceme an airy fairy effect! The leaves, soft and feathery, add to the delicate softness of the whole plant.

COLOR: Deep blue, lavender or white.
HEIGHT: 3 feet.
SEASON OF BLOOM: Summer.
LOCATION: Sunny fields, dry woodlands.
SOIL: Acid to neutral. Does best in deep, fertile soil.
TRANSPLANTING TIME: Early spring or early fall.
PROPAGATION: Seed.
MAY PICK.
RANGE: Pennsylvania to Minnesota, south to Georgia and Arkansas.

PICKERELWEED (*Pontederia cordata*). Pickerelweed Family
Stiff blossom spike covered with small blue florets, each one touched with a chartreuse dot. The spikes emerge from a long sheath around each stem. Heart-shaped leaves have interesting and rhythmic swirls of green lines. Botanical name is for Giulio Pontederia, a botany professor at Padua University in 1730. Beloved by deer in shallow mountain lakes and ponds where it grows. Seeds are nutlike, starchy and good to eat.
COLOR: Violet-blue.
HEIGHT: 1 to 3 feet.
SEASON OF BLOOM: August to September.
LOCATION: At edge of ponds or shallow shores of lakes or streams where water is not more than 12 inches deep.
SOIL: Wet mud.
TRANSPLANTING TIME: Early spring or early fall.
PROPAGATION: Lifting and dividing of rhizomes. Set in mud at bottom of pool. Rhizomes should not be disturbed for many years.
MAY PICK.
RANGE: Nova Scotia to Florida and Texas.

SPIKED LOBELIA (*Lobelia spicata*). Lobelia Family
Reaching up through the meadow grass on a sunny day are countless spires of this dainty fragile blossom of pale violet-blue. Slim leaves are almost toothless. When arranged in bouquets a few flower stems bring the essence of a soft June day indoors.
COLOR: Pale blue.
HEIGHT: 1 to 4 feet.
SEASON OF BLOOM: June to August.
LOCATION: Fields and meadows, in sunny, open areas.
SOIL: Moist or dry sandy soil.
TRANSPLANTING TIME: Spring or early fall.
PROPAGATION: Seed; division.
MAY PICK.
RANGE: Nova Scotia to Georgia, west to Minnesota and Arkansas.

WILD LUPINE (*Lupinus perennis*). Pea Family
Pealike violet-blue blossoms emerge in spike formation above soft hairy foliage. Each leaf is palmately divided, like that of the horse chestnut, into about eight narrow light-green leaflets. Related to the Texas Bluebonnet that flourishes by the mile along Western highways and is the state flower of Texas. Grows in sweeps in locust groves on Cape Cod. A legume, this establishes nitrogen in the soil and thus benefits all nearby growth.
COLOR: Blue.
HEIGHT: 1 to 2 feet.
SEASON OF BLOOM: May, June.
LOCATION: Dry, sunny woods.
SOIL: Needs sandy soil.

ASIATIC DAYFLOWER, WANDERING JEW (*Commelina communis*). Dayflower Family
Originally from Asia. Each flower lasts but a day. However, new ones keep unfolding. Often considered a common weed when the lance-shaped foliage wanders all through flower borders. But the bloom itself is a delight in its shape and pattern. Observe it closely with a magnifier to better appreciate the details. After a careful look you may be reluctant to dispose of this plant as an unwanted weed.

COLOR: Bright blue.
HEIGHT: 1 to 3 feet.
SEASON OF BLOOM: Summer and fall.
LOCATION: Widespread.
SOIL: Light, moist.
TRANSPLANTING TIME: Spring.
PROPAGATION: Cuttings; roots readily and rapidly, and self-sows.
SLIGHTLY FRAGRANT.
MAY PICK.
RANGE: Southern Canada, New York to Michigan and far south.

TRANSPLANTING TIME: Spring or fall. Difficult. You must take ample root soil along with the plant.
PROPAGATION: Best from seed sown when just ripe. Mix into your planting medium some soil in which lupines grew.
DON'T PICK.
RANGE: Nova Scotia, Quebec, Maine to Minnesota and south to the Gulf.

VIPERS' BUGLOSS, BLUEWEED (*Echium vulgare*). Borage Family
An ominous title for a charming flower. So named because the seeds were believed to be a remedy for snakebite. Naturalized here from Europe. Bristly hairy stems and hairy light-green leaves. Blossoms are tubular, with pink pistils and stamens. Buds often pink, opening to blue.

COLOR: Blue.
HEIGHT: 1 to 2 feet and higher.
SEASON OF BLOOM: Summer.
LOCATION: In old fields, sunny meadows, along roadsides.
SOIL: Prefers limestone and gravelly soil.
TRANSPLANTING TIME: Best to raise from seed.
PROPAGATION: Seed.
MAY PICK.
RANGE: Eastern and midland states and southern Canada.

BLUE CURLS, BASTARD PENNY-
ROYAL (*Trichostema dichotomum*).
Mint Family
The long blue stamens of this fragile
little flower grow outward in delightful
rhythmic swirls, hence one of its
common names. Leaves are narrow,
oblong, slightly sticky, and with the
scent of pennyroyal. The plant is an
old-time remedy used to heal wounds.

COLOR: Violet.

HEIGHT: 6 to 20 inches.

SEASON OF BLOOM: Summer and
fall.

LOCATION: Dry, sandy fields and
sunny meadows. Thrives in hot
summer.

SOIL: Dry, well-drained.

TRANSPLANTING TIME: This is an
annual, so best to raise from seed.

PROPAGATION: Seed.

MAY PICK.

RANGE: Maine to Florida, and
Missouri to Texas.

BOTTLE GENTIAN, CLOSED
GENTIAN (*Gentiana andrewsii*).
Gentian Family
Smooth green, pointed leaves form in
pairs all the way up the stalk. Closed
bottle-shaped deep-blue flowers are
clustered at the top; sometimes they
also emerge from the leaf bases. An
Illyrian king called Gentius first
discovered the medieinal value of the
Gentian's roots. The plant was named
in his honor. Old-time Indians used

these roots to make compresses to apply
to stiff and aching backs.

COLOR: Ultramarine blue.

HEIGHT: 1 to 2 feet.

SEASON OF BLOOM: Late summer
and fall.

LOCATION: Damp thickets and
woods, along streams.

SOIL: Moist loam best.

TRANSPLANTING TIME: Early
summer.

PROPAGATION: Best from seed,
planted in fall, with pans or flats exposed to frost and snow.

DON'T PICK.

RANGE: Eastern North America.

CHICORY, SUCCORY (*Cichorium
intybus*). Daisy Family
Along highways and waste areas stand
masses of these beautiful shaggy flowers.
They seem to reflect the various blue-
sky tones above. Especially deep-colored
at the seashore. Blossoms close in the
rain, open only on sunny days.
Blanched leaves may be used in salads

as you would use endive (another species of *Cichorium*). The roots may be ground and used as a coffee substitute or mixed with coffee.

COLOR: Violet-blue.
HEIGHT: 1 to 3 feet.
SEASON OF BLOOM: Summer and fall.
LOCATION: In full sun, everywhere, especially in waste places.
SOIL: Well-drained sandy loam.
TRANSPLANTING TIME: Spring; also late fall.
PROPAGATION: Seed; root cuttings in late fall.
MAY PICK.
RANGE: Widely naturalized from Europe in southern Canada and most of the United States.

GREAT LOBELIA (*Lobelia siphilitica*). Lobelia Family
A somewhat hairy plant whose leaves are pointed at both ends, irregularly toothed and with no stem. A number of attractive violet-blue flowers emerge all the way up the stalk. Named for Matthew de l'Obel, a Flemish botanist and physician to James I of England. De l'Obel was well-known for his horticultural knowledge, as were many physicians of earlier times. This plant was long in the pharmacopoea.

COLOR: Light blue-violet; some plants have deep blue-violet flowers.
HEIGHT: 1 to 3 feet.
SEASON OF BLOOM: Summer and fall.

LOCATION: Along streams, in marshes, wet pastures and thickets.
SOIL: Needs moist soil.
TRANSPLANTING TIME: Spring.
PROPAGATION: This species forms offsets in spring.
DON'T PICK.
RANGE: Maine to Louisiana.

HAREBELL, BLUEBELL
(*Campanula rotundifolia*). Bellflower Family
Native Harebell of England, and the famous Bluebells of Scotland. The delicate airy bluebells flower all across America and from sea level to one mile above. Especially prevalent through the White Mountains and the Rockies. Clings to steep cliffs, grows in dry spots and moist, in shade or sunshine. The name Harebell suggests that this variety grows in areas where hares abound.

COLOR: Blue-violet, varying from pale to rich tints.
HEIGHT: 6 to 18 inches.
SEASON OF BLOOM: Summer and fall.
LOCATION: Widespread across the country in almost all kinds of terrain, but especially on rocky slopes.
SOIL: Acid to neutral.
TRANSPLANTING TIME: Early spring.
PROPAGATION: Seed. Good for rock gardens.
MAY PICK.
RANGE: Arctic Circle southward to Appalachians and northern California.

IRONWEED (*Vernonia noveboracensis*). Daisy Family
Slightly tousled purple flower heads, suggesting those of the Aster (but actually lacking any ray flowers), cluster at the summit of a rough bristly plant. Many leaves crowd up the main stalk, slim, toothed, oval in shape and deep green. Latin name is for William Vernon, an English botanist and explorer of the seventeenth century. Called Ironweed because of the rigidity of the stem.
COLOR: Madder purple.
HEIGHT: 3 to 7 feet.
SEASON OF BLOOM: Summer and fall.
LOCATION: Moist, low fields and pastures, especially near the East Coast.
SOIL: Rich, sandy loam.

TRANSPLANTING TIME: Spring or fall.
PROPAGATION: Seed; underground stems. Best suited for sunny spots along edge of woods.
MAY PICK.
RANGE: Massachusetts to North Carolina and Mississippi, and locally north to the Great Lakes.

MARSH ROSEMARY, SEA LAVENDER, STATICE (*Limonium carolinianum*). Plumbago Family
A mist of lavender drifts over the beaches where this flower grows. Examine closely the leafless, many-branched stems, feathery with minute blossoms. A fragile-appearing plant, but one that withstands salt spray and ocean storms. Very popular in dried-flower arrangements.
COLOR: Lavender.
HEIGHT: 1 to 2 feet.
SEASON OF BLOOM: Summer and fall.
LOCATION: Along seacoasts, in salt meadows and marshes.
SOIL: Sandy, moist.
TRANSPLANTING TIME: Fall.
PROPAGATION: Seed (plant the dried flower clusters).
MAY PICK.
RANGE: Labrador to Texas on the coast.

NEW ENGLAND ASTER (*Aster novae-angliae*). Daisy Family
Creating a violet cloud along the late summer and fall roadsides, great clumps of these shaggy gypsy flowers flaunt their beauty. Defying the first frost, they bloom for weeks. Each blossom is the size of a quarter, with a golden disc center. Color varies from pale lilac to deep purple, depending on location and soil. Plant is stout-branched, rough and rugged. Beautiful to pick and arrange in a great vase beside your front door, where they are decorative and remain fresh for a long time.

COLOR: Purple-blue.
HEIGHT: 2 to 6 feet.
SEASON OF BLOOM: Summer and fall.
LOCATION: In moist and sunny meadows, swamps, along roadsides and streams, at edge of woods.
SOIL: Slightly acid or neutral.
TRANSPLANTING TIME: Spring or fall.
PROPAGATION: Division of clumps.
MAY PICK.
RANGE: Maine and Quebec to South Carolina and west to Colorado.

NIGHTSHADE, BITTER NIGHTSHADE (*Solanum dulcamara*).
Nightshade Family
Deep-purple starry flowers with vivid gold hearts (the anthers) are loosely gathered in among rich green triangular leaves. This is the Deadly Nightshade of legend and history. The drooping ruby-red berries are poisonous.

COLOR: Violet-purple.
HEIGHT: 2 to 8 feet, a shrubby climber.
SEASON OF BLOOM: Summer and fall.
LOCATION: Low, moist woodlands, waste areas, thickets.
SOIL: Sandy loam.
TRANSPLANTING TIME: Spring.
PROPAGATION: Seed.
DON'T PICK.
RANGE: Naturalized from Europe in eastern North America.

65

RABBIT'S-FOOT CLOVER
(*Trifolium arvense*). Pea Family
A soft fuzzy flower head, appealing as a small rabbit to touch and stroke. Triple light-green leaflets are narrow with blunt ends. A sweet-clover scent fills the area where these blossoms flourish. Thrives in waste places, poor gravelly soil, deserted pastures and barren stretches, as well as in cultivated fields.

COLOR: Warm gray-blue or gray.

HEIGHT: 4 to 10 inches.

SEASON OF BLOOM: Summer and fall.

LOCATION: Dry, sandy, rocky meadows and fields, along roadsides, in waste areas.

SOIL: Thrives in poor soil. Adaptable.

TRANSPLANTING TIME: This is an annual, so best to raise from seed.

PROPAGATION: Seed.

FRAGRANT.

MAY PICK.

RANGE: Eastern states, adventive (imperfectly naturalized) from Europe.

PURPLE CONEFLOWER
(*Echinacea purpurea*). Daisy Family
Another late-summer and autumn beauty to gather for bouquets indoors or out. The dark-purple-tufted cone-shaped center of the blossom is distinctive, and the many deep-violet toothed petals that droop around it add to the drama of this flower. Vies with the brilliant fall foliage for a place of honor along the roadsides and stone walls when summer ends.

COLOR: Deep purple varying to white.

HEIGHT: 2 to 5 feet.

SEASON OF BLOOM: Summer and fall.

LOCATION: Sunny fields and hillsides.

SOIL: Deep, fertile.

TRANSPLANTING TIME: Spring or fall.

PROPAGATION: Seed; lifting and separating rooted pieces. The roots go deep.

MAY PICK.

RANGE: Georgia north to Pennsylvania, westward and north to Minnesota.

WILD BERGAMOT (*Monarda fistulosa*). Mint Family
The shaggy, carefree, windblown blossoms send forth a deep and penetrating meadowy fragrance. Upper leaves are often stained with the pale-lilac tones of the flower bracts. The name *Monarda* honors Nicolas Monardes, a sixteenth-century physician and horticulturalist from Seville, Spain.

COLOR: Lavender.

HEIGHT: 2 to 3 feet.

SEASON OF BLOOM: Summer and fall.

LOCATION: Along roadsides, in sunny, moist fields and meadows, also dry ground.

SOIL: Acid to neutral.

TRANSPLANTING TIME: Spring or fall.

PROPAGATION: Seed; division of root clumps.

FRAGRANT.

MAY PICK.

RANGE: Southern Canada to Florida and Louisiana.

FRINGED GENTIAN (*Gentiana crinita*). Gentian Family

A special excitement of autumn is the Fringed Gentian. Blue as the October sky, the vase-shaped bud unfolds four softly fringed petals with a mysterious, misty quality about them. Opens only in the sunshine. Each bloom is white at the heart. Difficult to raise, but well worth trying. Simulate exactly conditions under which it grows in the wild and you will succeed.

COLOR: Blue.

HEIGHT: 1 to 3 feet.

SEASON OF BLOOM: Fall, after a light frost.

LOCATION: Wet meadows, damp thickets, dry, semi-shaded areas, brooksides.

SOIL: Varies from slightly acid to alkaline.

TRANSPLANTING TIME: Spring. A biennial. Roots break easily; growing from seed most practical.

PROPAGATION: Best from seed, planted in fall, with pans or flats exposed to frost and snow. Takes patience—the seeds are like delicate hairs.

DON'T PICK.

RANGE: Eastern North America and occasionally as far west as the Dakotas.

BELLWORT (*Uvularia sessilifolia*). Lily Family.

One of the easiest of all wildflowers to transplant and grow in your garden. Be sure to get the stalk beneath the earth and the creeping rhizome as well—you must dig deeper than you might expect. Nodding corn-yellow blossoms on a slim, drooping light-green plant. As blooms fade and new leaves develop, the whole plant changes character and becomes upright and broad. The seed capsule is charming, with three divisions separated by ridges.

COLOR: Corn yellow. Some are greenish yellow.

HEIGHT: 6 to 13 inches.

SEASON OF BLOOM: Spring.

LOCATION: In moist high and low thickets and woodlands.

SOIL: Acid, peaty.

TRANSPLANTING TIME: Spring or fall.

PROPAGATION: Seed; lifting and dividing rhizomes. Needs partly shaded area.

DON'T PICK.

RANGE: New Brunswick to Georgia, and Minnesota to Arkansas.

CALIFORNIA POPPY (*Eschscholtzia californica*). Poppy Family
State flower of California. From the midst of lacy light-green foliage crisp golden flowers appear. Each on its single stem looks as if made of freshly pressed tissue paper. Grows by the mile along the rugged coastline rising above the Pacific in areas around Carmel and Big Sur. Its botanical name honors Johann F. von Eschscholtz, a nine-teenth-century professor of medicine who traveled with a Russian expedition to California in 1815.

    COLOR: Yellow-orange.
    HEIGHT: 1 to 2 feet.
    SEASON OF BLOOM: Spring.
    LOCATION: In sunny fields.
Thrives in warm climates.
    SOIL: Light, sandy.
    TRANSPLANTING TIME: Spring or fall.
    PROPAGATION: Seed.
    DON'T PICK.
    RANGE: Originally Oregon and California; has spread into Nevada, Utah, New Mexico, Arizona—and even to southern Europe!

BLUE COHOSH (*Caulophyllum thalictroides*). Barberry Family
Interesting purple-blue leaves emerge from the soil in early spring. One compound leaf is three times divided, the leaflets each having three lobes. Young plant is dusted with a white "bloom" that disappears in maturity. A loose cluster of rich blue berrylike seeds follows the small six-pointed starry gold flowers. The blossoms stand out in deep woodlands through the late summer and fall.

    COLOR: Greenish yellow.
    HEIGHT: 1 to 3 feet.
    SEASON OF BLOOM: Spring.
    LOCATION: In deep woods and moist thickets.
    SOIL: Acid to neutral.
    TRANSPLANTING TIME: Spring or fall. Roots are poisonous.
    PROPAGATION: Seed; it self-sows readily.
    DON'T PICK.
    RANGE: Southeast Canada to Alabama and Mississippi.

SMALL YELLOW LADY'S-
SLIPPER (*Cypripedium parviflorum*).
Orchid Family
Narrow brown petals and sepals are
twisted in rhythmic curves as they
reach up and outward. Pendent in front
of them is the satiny yellow pouch
streaked with red-purple. Deeply lined
light-green leaves alternate up the stalk,
and the blossom rises at the top. An
illustrious and charming member of the
Orchid Family. If the plant likes your
conditions it will multiply and develop
into a colony. Give an autumn mulch
of oak leaves and pine needles. Certain
soil bacteria essential to the plant's
welfare will grow if such a mulch is
supplied.

    COLOR: Deep yellow.
    HEIGHT: 12 to 18 inches.
    SEASON OF BLOOM: May to July.
    LOCATION: High and low thickets,
wet woods, streamsides and bogs,
chiefly in the mountains.
    SOIL: Acid to neutral.
    TRANSPLANTING TIME: Early
spring. Take ample soil with roots.
These are close to the surface but
spread out.
    PROPAGATION: Root cuttings.
    FRAGRANT.
    DON'T PICK.
    RANGE: Quebec to Manitoba and
northern United States.

SUNDROP, EVENING PRIMROSE
(*Oenothera fruticosa*). Evening primrose Family
Fascinating reddish tapering buds open
into deep-golden flowers with orange
stamens. Blooms for a long period.
Blossoms last but a day, but more keep
coming. The roots of young plants are
edible and slightly resemble the parsnip
in flavor. Each bloom emerges where
leaves join the main stem.
    COLOR: Yellow.
    HEIGHT: 1 to 3 feet.
    SEASON OF BLOOM: June to July.
    LOCATION: Sunny fields and
meadows.
    SOIL: Sandy, not too dry.
    TRANSPLANTING TIME: Spring.
    PROPAGATION: Seed; division every
third year.
    MAY PICK.
    RANGE: Nova Scotia to South
Carolina, west to Missouri, Minnesota;
also occurs in Idaho.

DOG'S-TOOTH VIOLET,
YELLOW ADDER'S TONGUE,
TROUT LILY, FAWN LILY
(*Erythronium americanum*). Lily
Family
A dainty flower like a small golden Lily
with reflexed petals swings from a
single stem along streambanks and in
damp woodlands. Often grows in large
colonies where the purple-mottled
leaves form an interesting earth cover
and background for the dancing yellow
blooms. One of its common names,
"Trout Lily," comes from the long
slim speckled leaves that suggest a
trout; also it blooms at trout-fishing
time! Transplants easily if native conditions are duplicated.

COLOR: Yellow with brown mark-
ings.
HEIGHT: 5 to 10 inches.
SEASON OF BLOOM: Spring.
LOCATION: In moist woods and
thickets, along streams.
SOIL: Acid, sandy, peaty.
TRANSPLANTING TIME: Late
summer, 2 to 4 inches deep, in shade.
PROPAGATION: Offsets; division of
bulbs.
DON'T PICK.
RANGE: Nova Scotia to Florida
and west to Arkansas.

MARSH MARIGOLD, COWSLIP
(*Caltha palustris*). Buttercup Family
I've seen these bordering brooks in
sunny meadows and along streambanks
in filtered shade. They must have their
roots moist. Easy to transplant and
establish if you have a running stream.
Set the roots in the shallows of a small
backwater or just along the damp
banks. Especially welcome as they are
among the first signs of spring. Its Latin
name, *Caltha*, refers to a cup, and
palus to a marsh—so we have a marsh
cup! When feeling adventurous, boil a
few unopened buds in several waters
and use as you would capers—very
interesting.

COLOR: Golden yellow.
HEIGHT: 8 to 15 inches.
SEASON OF BLOOM: Early spring.
LOCATION: In marshes and wet
meadows, along shallow streams.
SOIL: Acid to neutral.
TRANSPLANTING TIME: Early
spring.
PROPAGATION: Seed; division of
roots.
DON'T PICK.
RANGE: Newfoundland to Ne-
braska, south to South Carolina.

SCOTCH BROOM (*Cytisus sco-parius*). Pea Family

Small shrub naturalized from Europe, including the Mediterranean regions and around Greece. Flourishes by the seashore and also along the roadside in mountainous areas. Stalks of the stiff green foliage, when bound together, make a lovely brush for your porch or terrace. Golden pealike blossoms spread their rich tones all the way up the flower stalks. It is said that Henry VIII frequently drank a brew made of the vivid yellow flowers as a protection against illness.

COLOR: Yellow.

HEIGHT: 2 to 4 feet.

SEASON OF BLOOM: Mid-May to June.

LOCATION: Meadows and low woodlands, in full sun or semi-shade. Sand barrens along the East Coast.

SOIL: Light, well-drained, but not limy.

TRANSPLANTING TIME: Spring.

PROPAGATION: Seed, sown when ripe; cuttings in August.

MAY PICK.

RANGE: Naturalized in various places from Massachusetts to Virginia, California and British Columbia, chiefly along both coasts.

DANDELION (*Taraxacum officinale*). Daisy Family

A plant that is everywhere. It burgeons in your lawn, and I have seen acres of it in the alpine meadows of Switzerland, where it competes for recognition with the rare mountain flowers. A spectacular blossom when examined closely. Children make curls of the stalks. Italians eat the leaves, which abound in vitamin A in early spring. The seeds are of an airy lightness. A plant from Europe to be appreciated and to be allowed to live more often for its spring charm. The common European name is *Dent-de-lion*—"tooth of the lion."

COLOR: Yellow.

HEIGHT: 3 to 14 inches.

SEASON OF BLOOM: Spring, off and on during summer.

LOCATION: Widespread.

SOIL: Adaptable.

TRANSPLANTING TIME: Summer.

PROPAGATION: Seed. It can hardly be eradicated.

MAY PICK.

RANGE: Almost worldwide except in the tropics and deserts.

ROUGH-FRUITED CINQUEFOIL
(*Potentilla recta*). Rose Family
A rough, erect plant. Each oval leaf
divided into five parts, hairy beneath
and toothed. Appealing inch-wide
golden flowers with delicate fragile
petals. The name *Potentilla* comes
from the reputed medicinal potency of
the plant to reduce fevers. The ancients
believed fevers came from evil spirits,
and a plant that reduced fevers dis-
persed wicked spirits and was invaluable.

COLOR: Yellow.
HEIGHT: 1 to 2 feet.
SEASON OF BLOOM: June to
August.
LOCATION: Fields, meadows, along
roadsides, low to high altitudes.
SOIL: Prefers well-drained soil,
not rich.
TRANSPLANTING TIME: Spring or
early fall.
PROPAGATION: Seed.
DON'T PICK.
RANGE: Maine to Ontario, Illinois
and south to Virginia. Introduced from
Europe.

DWARF BUSH HONEYSUCKLE
(*Diervilla lonicera*). Honeysuckle
Family
Children love to suck the nectar from
the base of these single honey-colored
florets. And not only children. This
touch of sweetness enhances anyone's
walk through sunny meadows. The
seedpod is oblong with a beaked tip.
The dark olive-green leaves are oval,
sharp-pointed and slightly toothed.

COLOR: Yellow.
HEIGHT: 3 to 4 feet.
SEASON OF BLOOM: Spring and
summer.
LOCATION: Widespread.
SOIL: Thrives in ordinary garden
soil.
TRANSPLANTING TIME: Spring or
fall.
PROPAGATION: Suckers and under-
ground runners. Seed may be sown
when ripe.
FRAGRANT.
MAY PICK.
RANGE: Newfoundland to Sas-
katchewan, south to North Carolina.

MEADOW BUTTERCUP (*Ranun-
culus acris*). Buttercup Family
A well-known, well-loved flower found
everywhere in fields and meadows. The
blossom has glossy yellow petals and
grows on a somewhat hairy plant. A
beautiful bloom to pick and arrange
indoors with Daisies and Clover. Such a
bouquet brings you a deep-meadow
scent. An old-time custom is to hold a
blossom under the chin: If your chin is
tinted with the reflected gold you like
butter. I guess everybody likes butter—
or margarine!

COLOR: Yellow.
HEIGHT: 2 to 3 feet.

SEASON OF BLOOM: Spring and summer.
LOCATION: Widespread.
SOIL: Adaptable.
TRANSPLANTING TIME: Spring or fall.
PROPAGATION: Division of roots.
MAY PICK.
RANGE: Naturalized from Europe across Canada and most of the United States.

GOLDEN ALEXANDERS, EARLY MEADOW PARSNIP (*Zizia aurea*).
Carrot Family
Golden flowers in loose radiating clusters top the main stalk of this attractive plant. Light-green compound leaves usually have three divisions, the leaflets narrow, pointed, sharply toothed. A host to countless small, many-colored butterflies. Blossoms at Daisy time and lends itself to interesting bouquets.

COLOR: Golden yellow.
HEIGHT: 2 to 3 feet.
SEASON OF BLOOM: Spring and summer.
LOCATION: Sunny meadows, open fields, damp areas and roadsides.
SOIL: Adaptable.
TRANSPLANTING TIME: Spring or fall.
PROPAGATION: Seed.
MAY PICK.
RANGE: New Brunswick to Florida and Texas.

FALSE HEATHER, WOOLLY HUDSONIA (*Hudsonia tomentosa*).
Rock-rose Family
This downy plant and flower are found at the seashore creeping over sand dunes and barrens—also along the beaches of the Great Lakes region. This bushy little shrub whose stems are hoary with down has unusual scaly leaves clinging close to the plant stalk. Tiny golden blossoms crowd along the upper parts to open only on sunny days.

COLOR: Yellow.
HEIGHT: 5 to 10 inches.
SEASON OF BLOOM: Spring and summer.
LOCATION: Sandy banks along the seacoast, sandy pine barrens.
SOIL: Moderately acid, sandy.
TRANSPLANTING TIME: Summer.
PROPAGATION: Cuttings in summer. Difficult.
MAY PICK.
RANGE: New Brunswick to Virginia and Great Lakes shores.

COLOR: Yellow.

HEIGHT: Rises to surface of water 3 to 5 feet deep. Some leaves and all flowers are lifted above the surface.

SEASON OF BLOOM: Summer.

LOCATION: Still water of lake margins, ponds, slow streams, meadow bogs.

SOIL: Needs rich soil.

TRANSPLANTING TIME: Spring.

PROPAGATION: Division of rhizomes.

DON'T PICK.

RANGE: Southern Canada, Maine to Minnesota and southward. A rather similar species in California, Colorado and the Northwest.

FIVE-FINGER, CINQUEFOIL

(*Potentilla canadensis*). Rose Family Glossy saw-edged leaflets with five fingers background five-petaled miniature yellow blooms. Suggests a yellow-flowered wild strawberry with stems that weave their green embroidery over the earth.

COLOR: Yellow.

HEIGHT: To 12 inches, prostrate.

SEASON OF BLOOM: Spring and summer.

LOCATION: Sunny dry fields and meadows, barren stony roadsides.

SOIL: Prefers well-drained soil.

TRANSPLANTING TIME: Spring or early fall.

PROPAGATION: Seed; runners. Spreads rapidly.

DON'T PICK.

RANGE: New Brunswick to Georgia and Texas.

YELLOW POND LILY, SPATTER-DOCK (*Nuphar advenum*). Water Lily Family

In order to thrive, the Water Lily must have its roots deep down in swampy muck. Drawing strength and vitality from these black depths, it reaches up through clear or brackish water to float leaves on the surface and unfold flowers into pure air and sunlight. The fruit is shaped like a short-necked bottle.

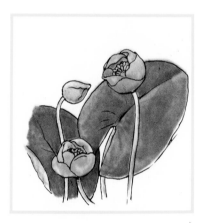

SWAMP BUTTERCUP (*Ranunculus septentrionalis*). Buttercup Family

The Buttercup Family is vast and illustrious. Every member has some particular charm. The foliage of this one is deeply indented, flower petals glossy. It blooms a little later than the meadow Buttercup and, characteristically, in swamps and low places. Stems are smooth and hollow. Each leaf is divided into three leaflets and each leaflet is three-lobed.

COLOR: Deep yellow.

HEIGHT: 1 to 2 feet.

SEASON OF BLOOM: Late spring and summer.

LOCATION: Low, sunny meadows, wet woods, marshes.

SOIL: Slightly acid.

TRANSPLANTING TIME: Spring to September.

PROPAGATION: Division or offsets.

MAY PICK.

RANGE: New Brunswick to Georgia and west to Kansas.

STAR GRASS (*Hypoxis hirsuta*). Amaryllis Family
If gold stars catch your eye as you wander through a deep grassy meadow, they can well be this pixie flower! The rich green grasslike leaves are covered with fine hair, and so are the flower buds that are greenish on the outside. A wild relative of the Daffodil.

COLOR: Yellow.

HEIGHT: 3 to 10 inches.

SEASON OF BLOOM: Spring and summer.

LOCATION: Sunny fields, pastures, open woods and woods trails.

SOIL: Light, sandy, peaty.

TRANSPLANTING TIME: Early spring.

PROPAGATION: Offsets.

DON'T PICK.

RANGE: Maine to Florida and Texas.

SEA MUGWORT, ARTEMISIA
(*Artemisia caudata*). Daisy Family
The attractive silvery-gray foliage is soft as velvet to touch. Another plant that thrives on the windy stretches of Cape Cod beaches and is prevalent along the East Coast shoreline everywhere. The foliage is a delight in flower arrangements. It is said to repel gnats, flies and "no-see-'ems." Flower heads very small, in wandlike panicles.

COLOR: Yellow.

HEIGHT: 2 to 5 feet.

SEASON OF BLOOM: Summer.

LOCATION: Seashore, salt marshes, also inland in stony ground.

SOIL: Will thrive even on poor dry soil.

TRANSPLANTING TIME: Early spring.

PROPAGATION: Seed.

MAY PICK.

RANGE: Atlantic coast, west to Manitoba and the Midwest.

BUTTERFLY WEED, PLEURISY
ROOT *(Asclepias tuberosa)*. Milkweed
Family
One of the loveliest and most exciting
of all wildflowers. The startling deep-
orange tones stand out in the meadows
and on banks where it flourishes. A
most sociable plant, for it is attractive
to countless butterflies of all sorts,
colors and sizes. Each floret is a work
of art, with both sharply reflexed petals
and upright petals. The florets are
grouped together into a great head of
bloom. In fall, graceful slender pods
burst open to float the seeds far and
wide.

COLOR: Yellow or orange.
HEIGHT: 1 to 3 feet.
SEASON OF BLOOM: Summer.
LOCATION: Dry fields and mead-
ows, roadsides.
SOIL: Light, dry, sandy or
gravelly, always in full sun.
TRANSPLANTING TIME: Spring or
fall; only young plants transplant well.
PROPAGATION: Seed, planted in
fall.
DON'T PICK.
RANGE: Maine to Florida and
west to Arizona.

CANADA LILY, YELLOW
MEADOW LILY *(Lilium canadense)*.
Lily Family
The first time you see a Canada Lily
you must stop your car, get out and go
close, or if you are walking, pause to
appreciate. This is among the most
beautiful of the sunny-meadow wildflowers. A plant with its own private
orchestra, for it is never free from the
hum of myriads of bees in all sizes and
varieties. Several blooms grow on a
single main stalk. Their nodding habit
of growth protects the nectar from rain.
Slim lance-shaped leaves grow in circles
up the stem. Flowers top the plant.

COLOR: Buff yellow, spotted
purple-brown.
HEIGHT: 2 to 5 feet.
SEASON OF BLOOM: June to July.
LOCATION: Widespread in fields,
swamps, meadows.
SOIL: Acid.
TRANSPLANTING TIME: Fall.
PROPAGATION: Seed; separating

groups of bulbs. Plant bulbs six to eight inches deep in lime-free loam or a mixture of sandy peat and leaf mold.

DON'T PICK.

RANGE: Southeastern Canada and Northeastern states. A form with redder flowers grows in Midwest states and the Appalachians.

DAYLILY (*Hemerocallis fulva*). Lily Family

Part of our early-summer floral drama is the common Daylily. Growing in great drifts of tawny orange, it is found along country roads and lanes. Though native to Europe and Asia, it is thoroughly at home here. Topping each flower stalk are seven or eight buds that open in succession. The ribbonlike leaves appearing in abundance taper to a sharp point. The name is from the Greek meaning "beautiful for a day," as each bloom lasts but a day. Newly opened blossoms may be boiled and buttered and served as a vegetable for dinner or dipped in batter and made into fritters—very interesting and delicious. You can also boil or fry the tubers; they taste rather like corn.

COLOR: Tawny orange.

HEIGHT: 2 to 5 feet.

SEASON OF BLOOM: Midsummer.

LOCATION: In meadows and old cemeteries, along streams and roads, at edge of woods.

SOIL: Should be well drained.

TRANSPLANTING TIME: Spring or fall.

PROPAGATION: Separation of rootstock.

MAY PICK.

RANGE: Southern Canada to Florida and Louisiana and west to Minnesota.

CANADA HAWKWEED (*Hieracium canadense*). Daisy Family

Like small Dandelions these flowers sweep through meadows and waste places. Clusters of buds grow at the tip of a downy stalk. In fall the plant is enhanced by a fringe of brown globes of down that drift through the air, carrying the seeds and spreading the species. An orange variety is *H. aurantiacum*, the Devil's Paintbrush, with hairy leaves, a beautiful plant heartily hated by Canadian and New England farmers.

COLOR: Yellow.

HEIGHT: 1 to 2 feet.

SEASON OF BLOOM: July to September.

LOCATION: Widely distributed.

SOIL: Adaptable.

TRANSPLANTING TIME: Spring or fall.

PROPAGATION: Seed, division.

DON'T PICK.

RANGE: Newfoundland to British Columbia, Oregon to New York and southern Pennsylvania.

DOWNY FALSE FOXGLOVE
(*Gerardia flava*). Snapdragon Family
Topping soft and velvety foliage, flower
spikes emerge. Gold trumpetlike florets
unfold all the way up each stalk, flowers
that are irresistible to the peacock
butterfly and countless bumblebees.
Foliage is yellow-green. Leaf stalks are
magenta-tinged. Named in honor of the
great herbalist John Gerarde, head
gardener to Lord Burghley, Minister of
State under Queen Elizabeth.
  Color: Rich yellow.
  Height: 2 to 4 feet.
  Season of bloom: Summer.
  Location: In fields, dry woods,
thickets, along roadsides.
  Soil: Somewhat acid.
  Transplanting time: September,
but only with associated plants.
  Propagation: Difficult. Plant is
parasitic on oak roots.
  Don't pick.
  Range: Eastern and Central
states.

EVENING PRIMROSE (*Oenothera biennis*) Evening Primrose Family
At dusk the large, showy, pure yellow
flowers open to send far and wide the
scent of sweet lemons. The blossom is
fertilized during the evening hours by

countless fascinating moths, including
the Isabella tiger-moth. If you are
patient and would like to see a wonder-
ful natural phenomenon, watch these
blossoms open just before the sun sets.
They remain wide open until the strong
sun of the following morning. An easy
plant to lift and grow in your garden.
  Color: Pure yellow.
  Height: 1 to 3 feet.
  Season of bloom: Summer.
  Location: Sunny fields and
meadows, along roadsides.
  Soil: Dry, sandy soil best.
  Transplanting time: Fall.
  Propagation: Seed. Self-sowing
once planted.
  Fragrant.
  May pick.
  Range: This or related species
found in most states of the Union and
in lower Canada.

LOOSESTRIFE, SWAMP CANDLE
(*Lysimachia terrestris*). Primrose
Family
A cloud of gold hovers over the
meadow where these small and lovely
five-petaled flowers grow. They form a
rather long open raceme, each flower
on a delicate horizontal stem. Leaves,
sharply pointed at either end, are long

and slim and often sepia-dotted. Makes a beautiful indoor summer bouquet of misty yellow.

COLOR: Yellow.
HEIGHT: 1 to 2 feet.
SEASON OF BLOOM: Summer.
LOCATION: Marshes, moist pastures, swamps.
SOIL: Should be damp.
TRANSPLANTING TIME: Spring or fall.
PROPAGATION: Division.
MAY PICK.
RANGE: Newfoundland to Georgia and westward.

MONEYWORT, CREEPING CHARLIE, CREEPING JENNY (*Lysimachia nummularia*). Primrose Family

Originally from Europe, this appealing vine creeps and trails. The shiny dark-green, almost round leaves on pendulous stems will spill most attractively out around the edge of a hanging basket on your porch or terrace. Stems grow to twenty inches. Dazzling gold flowers unfold up the stalk between leaf and stem. The name Moneywort comes from the round leaf, which suggests a small coin.

COLOR: Yellow.
HEIGHT: 1 to 3 feet.
SEASON OF BLOOM: Summer.
LOCATION: Damp grassy fields and pastures.
SOIL: Adaptable.
TRANSPLANTING TIME: Any time. Easy to grow.
PROPAGATION: Division. Does well in town gardens. Good for hanging baskets and window boxes.
FRAGRANT.
MAY PICK.
RANGE: Eastern Canada and throughout United States.

RATTLEBOX (*Crotalaria sagittalis*).
Pea Family
Opening pealike flowers and black
seedpods are both on the plant at the
same time. The hard dry seeds in their
inflated capsules rattle when blown by
a breeze or touched, hence the common name. Blooms are less than half
an inch long. Leaves are soft, hairy,
simple.
COLOR: Yellow.
HEIGHT: 4 to 12 inches.
SEASON OF BLOOM: Summer.
LOCATION: Sunny meadows and
roadsides.
SOIL: Dry, sandy soil.
TRANSPLANTING TIME: An annual; not practical to transplant.
PROPAGATION: Seed.
MAY PICK.
RANGE: Massachusetts and Vermont to Florida and Texas and north-
ward to South Dakota.

TURK'S-CAP LILY (*Lilium super-
bum*). Lily Family
A flower of elegance that stands out in
sunny wet meadows, bog margins, or
along partly shaded roadsides. The
reflexed segments expose handsome
stamens tipped with brown. Six to
eighteen pendent flowers appear in a
terminal pyramid. The blossom shape
strongly suggests a sultan's head-
dress. Monarch butterflies are drawn to

the nectar and hover over the blooms
on sunny days.
COLOR: Buff-orange to vermilion
spotted inside with brown.
HEIGHT: 3 to 7 feet.
SEASON OF BLOOM: July and
August.
LOCATION: Widespread, but not
quite as abundant as the Canada Lily.
Prevalent in coastal areas.
SOIL: Acid. Sun or half shade.
TRANSPLANTING TIME: Fall, 6 to
9 inches deep.
PROPAGATION: By offsets, bulb
scales.
DON'T PICK.
RANGE: New Brunswick to
Georgia and Missouri.

YELLOW MOUNTAIN
SAXIFRAGE (*Saxifraga aizoides*)
Saxifrage Family
An inhabitant of wet mountain ledges
as well as damp meadows and hillsides.
The attractive small twiggy plant bears
brown or deep-green stems and tooth-
less smooth slim leaves. Starry gold
flowers with orange centers cover the
greenery as it creeps and clings along
the damp rock outcroppings.
COLOR: Yellow.
HEIGHT: 2 to 7 inches.
SEASON OF BLOOM: Summer.
LOCATION: Glacial debris, mo-

raines, cold streambanks, wet rocks and
ledges.
   Soil: Moist and stony.
   Transplanting time: Spring or
early fall.
   Propagation: Seed; cuttings;
division of roots.
   Don't pick.
   Range: Arctic North America and
southward at high elevations.

BLACK-EYED SUSAN, CONE-
FLOWER (Rudbeckia hirta). Daisy
Family
One of the loveliest of all wildflowers—
a favorite of young and old. Beautiful
in bouquets, brilliant and exciting,
spreading in masses through sunny
pastures. If you own a field, scatter
seeds, along with Daisy and Clover
seeds, and the combination will bring
you a special summer beauty. Stems
and leaves are rough and bristly. This
flower is cross-fertilized not only by
insects but by the wind. Named in
honor of the famed Swedish botanists
Olaf Rudbeck and his son Olaf.
   Color: Rays golden yellow; disc
purple-brown.
   Height: 2 to 3 feet.
   Season of bloom: Summer and
fall.
   Location: Sunny fields and
meadows, from East to West.
   Soil: Should be fairly dry.

   Transplanting time: Spring or
fall. Plants can be moved easily.
   Propagation: Seed. A biennial
plant in nature. Seeds germinate in
late summer, winter over as young
plants and bloom the next year. May
be grown on same schedule in garden
or grown as annuals to bloom first year
by sowing indoors in spring and transplanting to garden after danger of
frost is past.
   May pick.
   Range: Virtually countrywide;
especially fine on dry plains.

BUTTER-AND-EGGS, TOADFLAX
(*Linaria vulgaris*). Snapdragon Family
Settle in the meadow some sunny day
in front of this gay, cheery little two-
lipped plant with its single long spur.
Here you must wait for a bee. The
creature will hum to a pause on the
blossom's lower lip. This swings open
with his weight, and the bee crawls in
for a sip and backs out pollen-covered.
A delightful process to observe. One of
the plant's common names comes from
the shades of the two-toned flower,
part butter yellow and part egg-yolk
orange.
  COLOR: Yellow and orange.
  HEIGHT: 1 to 3 feet.
  SEASON OF BLOOM: Summer and
fall.
  LOCATION: Common everywhere
in sunny fields and along roadsides.
  SOIL: Adaptable.
  TRANSPLANTING TIME: Spring or
fall.
  PROPAGATION: Seed. A free
seeder that spreads rampantly. Best for
wild garden.
  MAY PICK.
  RANGE: Across Canada and most
of the United States.

CLAMMY GROUND-CHERRY
(*Physalis heterophylla*). Nightshade
Family
Don't be thrown off by the name!
Sticky, hairy stems, broad heart-
shaped leaves, toothed and pointed.
Greenish-yellow flowers are cool and
fresh to view on a hot summer day.
Fruit is an inflated calyx enclosing a
yellow berry.
  COLOR: Green-yellow.
  HEIGHT: 1 to 3 feet, much
branched.
  SEASON OF BLOOM: Summer and
fall.
  LOCATION: Along roadsides, in
low woodlands.
  SOIL: Chiefly in sandy or alluvial
soil.
  TRANSPLANTING TIME: Spring or
early fall.
  PROPAGATION: Seed.
  MAY PICK.
  RANGE: New Brunswick south-
ward and westward.

COMMON SAINT-JOHN'S-WORT
(*Hypericum perforatum*). St. John's-
wort Family
Observe the many intriguing gold-
tipped pinlike stamens in each shiny
five-petaled blossom. Quantities of
flowers cover this gay plant of branching shape and healthy size. Leaves are
a dusky green, stemless and linear,
with translucent dots. In Scandinavia
in June, the month when witches held
nightly festivals, armfuls of these plants
were hung in the house and at the
entrance, as they were said to have the
power to ward off evil spirits. The
Italian name is *Cacciadiavolo*, exorcist.

COLOR: Golden yellow.

HEIGHT: 1 to 2 feet.

SEASON OF BLOOM: Summer and
fall.

LOCATION: Fields and waste land.

SOIL: Adaptable.

TRANSPLANTING TIME: Spring or
fall.

PROPAGATION: Runners. Should
not be planted in pastures where cattle
or horses graze as it is poisonous to
livestock. Can become a prolific weed.

FRAGRANT.

MAY PICK.

RANGE: Widely naturalized from
Europe through Canada and the
United States.

FEVER FLOWER, FERN-
LEAVED FALSE FOXGLOVE
(*Gerardia pedicularia*) Snapdragon
Family
Small golden bell-shaped flowers scattered among the fernlike foliage in late
summer and into fall. Sticky fine-hairy
leaves are cut into many lobes and are
nearly stemless. Both flowers and fruit
are most appealing. Fertilized by bumblebees and the light-brown butterfly
Junonia coenia.

COLOR: Yellow.

HEIGHT: 1 to 3 feet.

SEASON OF BLOOM: Summer and
fall.

LOCATION: Widespread in dry
thickets and woodlands.

SOIL: Dry. But plant is adaptable.

TRANSPLANTING TIME: This is an
annual or biennial, so transplanting is
not practical.

PROPAGATION: Difficult because
plant is parasitic. Will self-sow.

MAY PICK.

RANGE: Maine to Ontario, Minnesota and West Virginia.

GREAT MULLEIN (*Verbascum thapsus*). Snapdragon Family
Naturalized from Europe. Like a gold candle on the mountainsides of Switzerland, these flower spires rise up from a great rosette of gray-green leaves soft as rich velvet. A plant of stature, dignity and magnificence. In Roman army camps the soldiers used to dip the Mullein flower stalks into tallow and use them as torches. In remote areas the downy hairs are still sometimes used to make wicks.

COLOR: Yellow.

HEIGHT: 2 to 6 feet.

SEASON OF BLOOM: Summer.

LOCATION: Common in sunny fields, meadows, waste places, along rocky roadsides.

SOIL: Adaptable, but should be fairly dry.

TRANSPLANTING TIME: Spring or fall.

PROPAGATION: Seed. A biennial plant, best suited to wild gardens.

FRAGRANT.

MAY PICK.

RANGE: Widely spread across Canada and cooler areas of the United States.

CANADA GOLDENROD (*Solidago canadensis*). Daisy Family
Here is a plant naturalized in Europe from America. Often found cultivated in English perennial borders, where it is highly prized, and some fine horticultural hybrids have been created. A harbinger of early fall and a beautiful long-stemmed bloom to pick and arrange in tall bouquets outside your front door. Lasts many days in water. Leaves lance-shaped, toothed, dull olive green, slightly woolly beneath. The blossoms are in terminal panicles of many small heads on spaced-out arching stems.

COLOR: Golden yellow.

HEIGHT: 3 to 7 feet.

SEASON OF BLOOM: Late summer and fall.

LOCATION: Hillsides, meadows, edge of woods, streambanks, along stone walls.

SOIL: Acid.

TRANSPLANTING TIME: Fall.

PROPAGATION: Seed; division. Spreads rapidly.

MAY PICK.

RANGE: Newfoundland to Canadian Rockies and to Virginia and Tennessee. Most common species in Eastern states, and one of the finest.

HOP CLOVER(*Trifolium agrarium*).
Pea Family
As the dense little clusters of florets
wither and brown and fold downward
they resemble dried hops, hence the
common name. When fresh, the
blooms are soft and pleasant to touch.
The leaflets come in threesomes, clover-
style. The species name in Latin means
"of open fields," indicating where it
is usually found.
    COLOR: Yellow.
    HEIGHT: 6 to 15 inches.
    SEASON OF BLOOM: Summer and
fall.
    LOCATION: Sunny fields and road-
sides.
    SOIL: Sandy.
    TRANSPLANTING TIME: Early
spring will work fairly well. This is an
annual.
    PROPAGATION: Seed.
    MAY PICK.
    RANGE: Nova Scotia to Virginia,
westward to Ontario and Iowa.
Naturalized from Europe.

JEWELWEED, TOUCH-ME-NOT
(*Impatiens biflora*). Balsam Family
Touch the seedpods and they spring
open, tossing their treasure far and
wide. Beloved by hummingbirds for
their nectar, beloved by children who
delight in popping out the seeds. The
cornucopia-shaped flowers have a long
curving spur. Countless blossoms appear on each tall and broad-spreading
plant. Rub the crushed leaves on the
skin if you have been in or near poison
ivy and the irritation probably won't
develop.
    COLOR: Orange with small dark
spots; sometimes golden yellow.
    HEIGHT: 2 to 5 feet.
    SEASON OF BLOOM: Summer and
fall.
    LOCATION: In low woodlands,
along ditches, streams and wet shady
roadsides.
    SOIL: Acid.
    TRANSPLANTING TIME: Best
raised from seed. An invasive weed.
    PROPAGATION: Seed; self-sows.
Best for wild garden or partly shaded
border.
    MAY PICK.
    RANGE: Newfoundland to Florida
and west to Nebraska.

follow, which split open suddenly when ripe, throwing the seeds for several feet.
COLOR: Yellow.
HEIGHT: 1 to 2 feet.
SEASON OF BLOOM: July to September.
LOCATION: Widespread in sunny fields and meadows.
SOIL: Does best in dry, sandy soil.
TRANSPLANTING TIME: Spring.
PROPAGATION: Seed.
DON'T PICK.
RANGE: Massachusetts to Florida, west to South Dakota and New Mexico.

LANCE-LEAVED GOLDENROD (*Solidago graminifolia*). Daisy Family
This is the Goldenrod with slim downy ribbonlike leaves and tiny flower clusters forming flat heads in long compound bunches, unlike any other Goldenrod. A subtle fragrance suggesting new-mown hay. Stems wiry and stiff. Another wildflower that lasts many days in a tall vase of water on your terrace or porch.
COLOR: Golden yellow.
HEIGHT: 2 to 4 feet.
SEASON OF BLOOM: Summer and fall.
LOCATION: Widely distributed. Riverbanks, moist situations, damp woods.
SOIL: Acid.
TRANSPLANTING TIME: Early spring or fall.
PROPAGATION: Seed, division of roots.
FRAGRANT.
MAY PICK.
RANGE: New Brunswick to Florida and west to Nebraska.

PARTRIDGE PEA (*Cassia fasciculata*). Pea Family
A very sensitive plant whose leaves shrink back and fold up when touched, but open again later. Five-petaled showy flowers, three-fourths of an inch wide, and as deep-toned as pirate's gold, star the attractive soft, dark-green foliage. When the blossoms fade, interesting two-inch-long hairy pods

POOR-ROBIN'S-PLANTAIN, POOR-ROBIN'S-HAWKWEED, RATTLESNAKE WEED (*Hieracium venosum*). Daisy Family
The purple-veined light-green leaves are fascinating. Flowers like miniature Dandelions are soft and furry to touch. One popular name comes from the fact that the plant flourishes in areas where rattlesnakes are prevalent. *Hieracium* comes from the Greek word for hawk. Pliny used the stem juice as an eyewash and claimed it gave one the clear, sharp vision of a hawk.
COLOR: Golden yellow.
HEIGHT: 12 to 20 inches.
SEASON OF BLOOM: Summer.
LOCATION: Dry thickets and woodlands, often under pines.
SOIL: Adaptable. Does well in poor, sandy soil.
TRANSPLANTING TIME: Spring or fall.

PROPAGATION: Seed; lifting and dividing clumps. Sow seed in late spring or summer for blooms the following year.

MAY PICK.

RANGE: Maine to Georgia and west to Nebraska.

SOIL: Sandy.

TRANSPLANTING TIME: Spring or fall.

PROPAGATION: Seed; division of clumps.

MAY PICK.

RANGE: Nova Scotia to Florida.

COMMON SUNFLOWER
(*Helianthus annuus*). Daisy Family
The state flower of Kansas, where it burgeons along the highways. Revered by the Incas in Peru as an image of their sun god. Pizarro's men took back seeds to Spain. The seeds were, and are, a source of nutriment as well as of oil. Petals are used in making a color-fast yellow dye. The leaves are dried and often smoked in place of tobacco.

COLOR: Yellow.

HEIGHT: 2 to 10 feet.

SEASON OF BLOOM: Summer and fall.

LOCATION: In dry, sunny places.

SOIL: Adaptable.

TRANSPLANTING TIME: Early summer gives fairly good results; the plant is an annual.

PROPAGATION: Seed.

MAY PICK.

RANGE: Originally the Great Plains; now escaped from farms and gardens here and there across the country.

SEASIDE GOLDENROD (*Solidago sempervirens*). Daisy Family
Early fall is announced by great clumps of this golden flower. It stands in sweeps along the shores and beaches of Cape Cod and the whole Eastern Seaboard. The gold tones are rich and vibrant, the form and habit of the plant vital and strong. Attracts the migrating monarch butterflies. One of our magnificent plants. Watch for it every year on Connecticut shores and Fire Island.

COLOR: Golden yellow.

HEIGHT: 2 to 6 feet.

SEASON OF BLOOM: September to October.

LOCATION: Along sunny seashores and banks of tidal rivers. Salt marshes.

LOCATION: Widespread in the East in swamps and moist meadows and along roadsides.

SOIL: Prefers damp soil.

TRANSPLANTING TIME: Early summer, this sunflower, somewhat surprisingly, is perennial.

PROPAGATION: Seed.

MAY PICK.

RANGE: Northeastern and Central states and lower Canada.

FALL DANDELION (*Leontodon autumnalis*). Daisy Family

Basal leaves with jagged lobes background these fringed golden flowers that greet the autumn. Slender stems are wiry, not tubular as in the spring Dandelion. The Greek-Latin generic name means "lion's tooth."

COLOR: Golden yellow.

HEIGHT: 10 to 18 inches.

SEASON OF BLOOM: Late summer and fall.

LOCATION: Sunny fields and roadsides.

SOIL: Neutral, not rich, often stony.

TRANSPLANTING TIME: Early summer.

PROPAGATION: Offshoots or basal branches.

MAY PICK.

RANGE: Naturalized from Europe. Newfoundland to Ontario, Michigan and Pennsylvania.

GIANT SUNFLOWER (*Helianthus giganteus*). Daisy Family

Interesting and dramatic large heads of flowers that always turn toward the sun, following it from east to west through the day. Stalks of this plant were shredded and used as textile fibers by primitive people. Long, slim leaves of bright green are pointed and finely toothed and usually grow alternately up the stem.

COLOR: Light yellow.

HEIGHT: 3 to 12 feet.

SEASON OF BLOOM: Summer and fall.

WILD COLUMBINE (*Aquilegia canadensis*). Buttercup Family
Through the unspoiled rocky meadows of New England, the Adirondacks, the White Mountains, this fragile-appearing but hardy plant runs rampant. Here the two-toned red-and-yellow flowers swinging on delicate stems in every breeze are host to hummingbirds, bees, moths and butterflies. They are beloved by children for their gay colors and interesting shape. The petals are five tubes tapering back into spurs. *Columba*, in Latin, means "dove." An ancient Roman gardener with a vivid imagination saw in an Italian species five doves perched around a circle, hence the name.

COLOR: Yellow and scarlet.
HEIGHT: 1 to 2 feet.
SEASON OF BLOOM: April to June.
LOCATION: In shaded rocky areas and woodlands, occasionally in open fields.
SOIL: Thrives in ordinary garden soil, acid to neutral, but moist loam best.
TRANSPLANTING TIME: Early spring or early fall.
PROPAGATION: Seed for blooms the following year; lifting and separating plants. When old plants start to deteriorate, raise fresh ones from seed. Among the easiest to get started in a new area.
DON'T PICK.
RANGE: Nova Scotia to Florida and Texas. Related species in the West.

MOCCASIN FLOWER, PINK LADY'S-SLIPPER. (*Cypripedium acaule*). Orchid Family
From deep between two lined and pointed leaves rises a single stalk topped by the fabulous Pink Lady's-Slipper, one of our most appealing wild Orchids. The central pink pouch is veined with deeper pink surrounded by brown wavy and curved petals and sepals. When you have transplanted some plants to your woodland garden be sure to mulch each autumn with oak leaves and pine needles. This ensures annual bloom.

COLOR: Crimson-pink.
HEIGHT: 8 to 12 inches.
SEASON OF BLOOM: Spring.
LOCATION: In sandy or rocky woods, usually under or near pine, hemlock or oak trees.
SOIL: Dry, acid.
TRANSPLANTING TIME: Early spring.
PROPAGATION: Difficult. Collect wild specimens (if they are numerous) for planting in the garden, duplicating as nearly as possible conditions under which they grew in nature.
DON'T PICK.
RANGE: Newfoundland to Winnipeg, south to North Carolina and Tennessee.

RED CLOVER (*Trifolium pratense*).
Pea Family
State flower of Vermont. Main characteristic is the three-lobed leaves, hence the name. Favorite of children and adults. Lovely in early summer bouquets combined with Daisies. Sweet meadowy scent. Pull out a few florets and suck the bases for a honey-rich flavor. Seldom is the plant free from the hovering bumblebees that fertilize it. Clovers, and most of the Pea Family, are valuable for releasing nitrogen to the soil and thus to surrounding plants. Clover played an important part in the pagan rites of the Druids and Greeks. Clover is not only for clover honey; dry some flower heads and steep them in boiling water for a delicious tea.

COLOR: Dusty magenta or deep pink.
HEIGHT: 8 to 24 inches.
SEASON OF BLOOM: Early spring.
LOCATION: Along roadsides, in sunny, sandy meadows.
SOIL: Sandy.
TRANSPLANTING TIME: Spring or fall.
PROPAGATION: Seed; runners.
FRAGRANT.
MAY PICK.
RANGE: Naturalized from Europe over much of Canada and the United States.

SHOWY ORCHIS (*Orchis spectabilis*). Orchid Family
A beautiful Orchid of the woodland.

From between two glowing green leaves a flower spike rises bearing up the stem three to seven flowers, each with a purple-rose hood and white lip and spur. Visited and fertilized by the bumblebee.

COLOR: Magenta and white.
HEIGHT: 5 to 10 inches.
SEASON OF BLOOM: May–June.
LOCATION: Rich, low woodlands.
SOIL: Moderately acid, woodsy soil best.
TRANSPLANTING TIME: Early spring. Difficult to move. Take ample soil around roots. Settle in cool shade. Avoid hot, dry positions.
PROPAGATION: Seed.
DON'T PICK.
RANGE: New Brunswick south to Georgia and west to North Dakota and Missouri.

SPRING BEAUTY (*Claytonia virginica*). Purslane Family
Nodding buds, perky upright flowers, with flush of crimson-pink petals veined in deeper pink, a white center and gold stamens. The plant has sinuous, half-reclining stems and ribbonlike leaves. Both flowers and foliage are delicate and fresh as spring herself. Genus named in honor of John Clayton, an eighteenth-century American botanist who came to Virginia and studied numerous flowers.

COLOR: Pale pink or white.
HEIGHT: 6 to 12 inches.
SEASON OF BLOOM: Early spring.

LOCATION: In low, moist woodlands, sometimes along streams.
SOIL: Moderately acid.
TRANSPLANTING TIME: Early spring or fall.
PROPAGATION: Seed or division. Best in damp semi-shade in wild garden.
DON'T PICK.
RANGE: Eastern North America.

TRAILING ARBUTUS, MAYFLOWER (Epigaea repens). Heath Family

The Mayflower of New England. This blossom breathes the scent of spring, is spring itself in essence, and one of the most loved and coveted of all the first flowers of the new season. The plant creeps and spreads over north slopes of rocky woodlands. Hidden beneath the dull rust-spotted dark-green leaves of last season are small bundles of deep-pink buds that open early into dainty waxlike shell-pink flowers with an indescribably fresh fragrance. New light-green leaves open in June and are netted with fine veins. State flower of Massachusetts.
COLOR: Pink and white.
HEIGHT: 3 to 6 inches. Trailing.
SEASON OF BLOOM: Spring.

LOCATION: In woods and on rocky ledges, usually near evergreens.
SOIL: Acid, peaty or lime-free sandy loam.
TRANSPLANTING TIME: Fall; needs a winter mulch.
PROPAGATION: Layering; division. Difficult.
FRAGRANT.
DON'T PICK.
RANGE: Newfoundland to Florida and Kentucky.

WAKE-ROBIN, PURPLE TRILLIUM (Trillium erectum). Lily Family

Three graceful, broad-ovate, lined and pointed leaves form a whorl just below the mahogany-red flowers. Three petals are pointed and set on a rosette of three green sepals. Easy to transplant and soon settles and grows into a large colony in your woodland garden. This Purple Trillium attracts flies and has a carrion smell, but not too strong; it is the "Ill-scented Wake-robin."
COLOR: Maroon.
HEIGHT: 7 to 15 inches.
SEASON OF BLOOM: Early spring to June.

LOCATION: Woodlands and thickets, along stone walls.
SOIL: Acid loam. Add leaf mold or peat moss.
TRANSPLANTING TIME: Spring or early summer.
PROPAGATION: Seed; lifting and dividing clumps. Needs shade or semi-shade. Good for rock garden or wild garden.
DON'T PICK.
RANGE: Nova Scotia to Tennessee and Manitoba to Missouri.

WILD PINK (*Silene caroliniana*).
Pink Family
Fresh valentine-pink flowers, crisp and
charming, carpet the mountain
meadows throughout North Carolina,
Virginia, the whole Southern region.
Delicate five-petaled flowers terminate
the stems. The plant is attractive in
itself with slim pointed leaves of dark
green. Arrange in small bouquets for
dressers, entryways, bathrooms and
wherever space is limited.
COLOR: Rose-carmine, pink or
occasionally white.
HEIGHT: 10 inches.
SEASON OF BLOOM: Spring.
LOCATION: In meadows at edge of
woods. Needs sun.
SOIL: Dry, sandy.
TRANSPLANTING TIME: Early
spring or fall.
PROPAGATION: Seed. Good for
rock garden or wild garden. Self-sows.
MAY PICK.
RANGE: Eastern North America,
varying locally.

MOSS PINK (*Phlox subulata*). Phlox
Family
A plant like a mat of thick green moss
starred with countless pink and
magenta (and sometimes blue or white)
blooms. So abundantly does it blossom
that in the spring the foliage is totally
hidden by flowers. Folds over slopes,
stone walls, holds banks, deterring them
from washing out. Leaves sharp-tipped,
linear and close-set.
COLOR: Crimson. Subspecies and

cultivars vary from white to shades of
pink and blue.
HEIGHT: 2 to 5 inches.
SEASON OF BLOOM: Spring,
summer.
LOCATION: Dry, sunny fields, open
woodlands, along streambanks.
SOIL: Sandy loam.
TRANSPLANTING TIME: Spring or
early summer.
PROPAGATION: Seed; cuttings.
Easy to grow in sunny, well-drained
area. Excellent for wall gardens.
DON'T PICK.
RANGE: Quebec, Ontario, New
York to Michigan, south to North
Carolina and Kentucky.

ATAMASCO LILY, ZEPHYR LILY
(*Zephyranthes atamasco*). Amaryllis
Family
Grasslike leaves are a shiny, deep green.
The flower has six symmetrical stamens
and one pistil. The blossom cup has six
distinct lobes. The botanical name
comes from the Greek *zephyros* and
anthos, meaning "flower of the west
wind," and was given to the plant by
an English botanist because it was
brought to England from America,
figuratively, by the west wind; *atamasco*

is an Indian word meaning "stained with red," and suggests the tones of the bloom, often red-tinged.

COLOR: Pink or white tinged with magenta.
HEIGHT: 6 to 15 inches.
SEASON OF BLOOM: Spring, summer.
LOCATION: Damp meadows and woods.
SOIL: Light or sandy.
TRANSPLANTING TIME: Spring.
PROPAGATION: Seed; offsets.
DON'T PICK.
RANGE: Southeast Virginia to Florida and Alabama.

BEACH PEA, SEASIDE PEA
(*Lathyrus maritimus*). Pea Family
Appealing blue-green foliage with curling tendrils reaches to cling and twine. Ruddy purple flowers are pea-like. Flourishes in pure sand on the Eastern Coast beaches; also along the shores of the Great Lakes. Makes attractive early-summer indoor arrangements. Interesting seedpods are veiny and about two inches long. Named from the old Greek word for pea, *lathyrus*. You can eat the fresh young peas.

COLOR: Red-violet and red-purple.
HEIGHT: 1 to 2 feet.
SEASON OF BLOOM: Spring, summer.
LOCATION: Along seashore and in sandy fields close to the ocean.

SOIL: Sandy, neutral.
TRANSPLANTING TIME: Spring or fall.
PROPAGATION: Seed; division.
MAY PICK.
RANGE: New Jersey and Oregon north to the Arctic Sea; also the Great Lakes.

CORAL HONEYSUCKLE, TRUMPET HONEYSUCKLE
(*Lonicera sempervirens*). Honeysuckle Family
Informally called the Firecracker Vine. Attractive tubular blossoms resemble bunches of small coral-red firecrackers. Long fleshy leaves and stems of interesting blue-green wave about in the breeze, seeking fences and stone walls to sprawl over. Note how the roundish upper leaves encircle the stem. These are evergreen in the South. A favorite of the hummingbird, whose long slim bill can easily reach well into the heart of the flower.

COLOR: Coral pink.
HEIGHT: 8 to 15 feet, climbing.
SEASON OF BLOOM: Spring, summer.
LOCATION: Open woods and sunny meadows, fence rows, thickets.
SOIL: Slightly acid.
TRANSPLANTING TIME: Spring.
PROPAGATION: Seed; cuttings.
MAY PICK.
RANGE: Canada to Gulf of Mexico; also in the Rockies.

INDIAN PAINTBRUSH (*Castilleja lineariaefolia*). Snapdragon Family
A lusty, vivid, dramatic blossom whose flame tones, the brightest of reds, stand out among the sagebrush and on the dry prairie where it thrives. In the West children break the flower stems and gather the juice, which promptly firms up for a pleasant wild chewing gum. Named for Domingo Castillejo, a Spanish botanist. Other species grow in the high mountains of the Northwest, and one (*C. coccinea*) grows in damp sandy ground from Massachusetts to Tennessee and Texas.

COLOR: Salmon, red, purple.
HEIGHT: 1 to 2 feet.
SEASON OF BLOOM: Spring, summer.
LOCATION: Arid prairies and high, flat tablelands.
SOIL: Prefers sandy soil. Use equal parts of leaf mold, peat and loam with the sand.
TRANSPLANTING TIME: Spring.
PROPAGATION: Seed; division of clumps. Difficult to grow.
MAY PICK.
RANGE: Wyoming to New Mexico and California.

DRAGON'S-MOUTH, SWAMP PINK, WILD PINK (*Arethusa bulbosa*). Orchid Family
A delicately scented Orchid with a fascinating shape and design. The flower lip is recurved and spreading, spotted and fringed, making a beautiful landing platform for visiting insects, especially bumblebees, which are frequent visitors to this flower. The plant has a solitary leaf, long and slim, practically hidden in the sheathed scape. When flowering is over, this develops. Botanical name is for the fountain nymph Arethusa.

COLOR: Rose-purple.
HEIGHT: 5 to 10 inches.
SEASON OF BLOOM: Spring, summer.
LOCATION: Wet meadows and woodlands, bogs. Rather rare.
SOIL: Moist, cool, acid.
TRANSPLANTING TIME: Spring.
PROPAGATION: Offsets from bulb. Difficult to protect the bulb from rodents.
FRAGRANT: Like violets.
DON'T PICK.
RANGE: Newfoundland to Ontario and Minnesota; also in mountains of South Carolina.

PURPLE PITCHER PLANT, SIDE-SADDLE FLOWER (*Sarracenia purpurea*). Pitcher-plant Family
A fierce, carnivorous plant. The leaves are like pitchers and always half-filled with liquid. Their outer surface is smooth, but the inside is covered with bristling hairs pointing downward. Visiting insects have trouble escaping, fall into the fluid, are absorbed and contribute to the sustenance of the plant. The raw-meat color of the flower adds a further sinister note. The bloom is nodding to protect the pollen from the elements.

COLOR: Dull, dark red.
HEIGHT: 4 to 10 inches.
SEASON OF BLOOM: Spring and summer.
LOCATION: Grows in peaty bogs, swamps, low, moist woods. Flowers do not appear until the plant is several years old.

SOIL: Acid, moist.
TRANSPLANTING TIME: Early spring.
PROPAGATION: Seed; division.
DON'T PICK.
RANGE: Eastern North America.

WOOD BETONY, LOUSEWORT
(*Pedicularis canadensis*). Snapdragon Family

Don't be thrown off by that weird name Lousewort—both flowers and foliage are charming. Red and yellow blooms group themselves together on a cushion of fernlike leaves at the top of a stem. More leaves like little ferns emerge at the base of the blossom stalk. Flourishes in meadows and fields and along roadsides.

COLOR: Red and yellow.
HEIGHT: 6 to 10 inches.
SEASON OF BLOOM: Spring and summer.
LOCATION: Sunny meadows, dry, open woodlands.

SOIL: Acid to neutral.
TRANSPLANTING TIME: September.
PROPAGATION: Seed; division.
Difficult to grow. Best in a wild garden.
MAY PICK.
RANGE: Nova Scotia to Manitoba and southward.

BOUNCING BET, SOAPWORT
(*Saponaria officinalis*). Pink Family
Naturalized from Europe. Scallop-tipped petals. Delicious old-fashioned spicy fragrance. Flowers grow in clusters at the top of the stem. Found in great drifts on Nantucket, stretches along many of the highways through the Rockies. Bouncing Bet is an ancient English term for Bouncing Elizabeth. Which Elizabeth, one wonders? Latin name is from *sapo*, meaning soap. One English writer about plants calls it Soapy Sam. Leaves, when bruised and put in water, produce soapy lather.

COLOR: Magenta, pink, white.
HEIGHT: 1 to 3 feet.
SEASON OF BLOOM: Summer.
LOCATION: In open, sunny fields and meadows, ditches beside roads, railway embankments.
SOIL: Adaptable.
TRANSPLANTING TIME: Spring or fall.
PROPAGATION: Seed; division.
Self-sows freely.
FRAGRANT.
MAY PICK.
RANGE: Across the United States in temperate, not too dry areas.

FIREWEED, SPIKED WILLOW-
HERB (*Epilobium angustifolium*).
Evening Primrose Family
A flower found in many countries in
the north temperate zones. Springs up
in burned-over areas. Grows by the
mountainside in Switzerland, likewise
in the Rockies and in countless areas in
between. Interestingly, you find bud,
flower and seedpod on the plant
simultaneously. Leaves resemble those
of the willow. Down-tufted seeds are
carried on the breeze great distances
and so spread the species. Early spring
shoots may be eaten like asparagus.
In England the dried leaves are often
mixed with tea.
> COLOR: Magenta.
> HEIGHT: 4 to 7 feet.
> SEASON OF BLOOM: Summer.
> LOCATION: Widespread, often
appearing in woodlands after they have
been burned over or cleared.
> SOIL: Acid to neutral, dry and
sandy.
> TRANSPLANTING TIME: Fall.
> PROPAGATION: Seed; division of
rooted pieces. Good in a wild garden.
> MAY PICK.
> RANGE: Canada, Alaska,
Montana, Colorado, Northwest.

FLAMING SWORD, OCOTILLO,
COACHWHIP (*Fouquieria splendens*).
Candlewood Family
This spiny shrub flourishes in the
desert areas of Arizona, California and
New Mexico. The formidable stalk
is covered for short periods after the
rains with smooth, round light-green
leaves. Overnight, and as a complete
surprise, the soft delicate feathery
flowers in flaming orange-red appear.
The blossom stalks wave back and
forth in the breeze like flaming flags
against the desert sand. Later the dry
woody stems can be lighted like candles.
> COLOR: Red.
> HEIGHT: 6 to 15 feet.
> SEASON OF BLOOM: April, May.
> LOCATION: Dry deserts of the
West.
> SOIL: Well drained.
> TRANSPLANTING TIME: Spring.
> PROPAGATION: Cuttings.
> DON'T PICK.
> RANGE: See above.

MAIDEN PINK (*Dianthus deltoides*).
Pink Family
Small fringed flowers rise up from
silvery-green mat-forming plants. Found
in abundance around old deserted
houses and in ancient New England
cemeteries. Leaves ribbon-slim and
pointed. Blossoms send out the scent of
cloves and spices. In the sunshine after
a rain the fragrance travels far and wide
in the places where the flowers bloom.
> COLOR: Crimson-pink.
> HEIGHT: 6 to 12 inches.
> SEASON OF BLOOM: May–June.

LOCATION: Sunny meadows and pastures.

SOIL: Adaptable, but prefers well-drained soil, not too acid.

TRANSPLANTING TIME: Early fall.

PROPAGATION: Seed; cuttings; layering. The plants spread freely and live long.

FRAGRANT.

MAY PICK.

RANGE: Naturalized in many parts of the United States.

MARSH PINK (*Sabatia dodecandra*). Gentian Family

The attractive two-inch-wide pink blossoms have gay golden centers. The basal leaves are blunt-tipped and tapered toward the bottom. The foliage on the upper part of the plant is light green and becomes slim and lance-shaped. The stems are four-angled. Genus named for Liberato A. Sabati, an eighteenth-century Italian botanist. Asa Gray called this one of the handsomest plants in America. It used to grow near Jones Beach, New York, and probably still does in remote parts of the meadows; also near Morehead City, North Carolina.

COLOR: Deep rose.

HEIGHT: 1 to 2 feet.

SEASON OF BLOOM: Summer.

LOCATION: In moist, sunny areas, salt meadows, swamps, along the seacoast.

SOIL: Should be damp.

TRANSPLANTING TIME: Spring.

PROPAGATION: Seed, sown in late spring, with seedlings kept in cold frame over winter and planted in permanent position the following spring.

MAY PICK.

RANGE: Massachusetts to North Carolina.

MEADOWSWEET (*Spiraea latifolia*). Rose Family

A foam of pink flowers, like apple blossoms in miniature, crowd the reddish stems of this wayside shrub. The fragrant blossom plume is feathery and soft to touch. In olden times the blooms were used in garlands and wreaths.

COLOR: Flesh pink.

HEIGHT: 2 to 4 feet.

SEASON OF BLOOM: Summer.

LOCATION: In old meadows, open woods, rocky areas, along roadsides.

SOIL: Slightly acid.

TRANSPLANTING TIME: Spring or fall.

PROPAGATION: Seed; division.

FRAGRANT.

MAY PICK.

RANGE: Newfoundland to Virginia.

SPIKED LOOSESTRIFE, PURPLE LOOSESTRIFE (*Lythrum salicaria*).
Loosestrife Family
Grows in abundance along the marshy shores of the Hudson River, the Delaware and in the swamps of Wallkill Valley. Borders the Housatonic River in Connecticut. Adapts to being moved and will grow readily on your land if you give it favored conditions. The leaf suggests the willow leaf, long and slim. The Greek generic name means "blood" and alludes to the styptic character of the plant. Horticultural hybrids are popular modern garden plants.

COLOR: Magenta.
HEIGHT: 2 to 3 feet.
SEASON OF BLOOM: July to September.
LOCATION: Sunny, wet places, low spots near water, swamps.
SOIL: Neutral, moist.
TRANSPLANTING TIME: Early spring or fall.
PROPAGATION: Separation of rooted pieces from the outside of root clumps. If possible, avoid lifting entire root clump, since the plant will then require another year to become reestablished.
MAY PICK.
RANGE: Naturalized from Europe in Eastern and Central states.

SHEEP LAUREL, LAMBKILL
(*Kalmia angustifolia*). Heath Family
Named Lambkill because the plant is poisonous to livestock. Common in meadows and fields where sheep graze. Evergreen leaves and flowers resemble mountain laurel but are smaller. Newer leaves standing upright terminate the stems. An encircling flower cluster develops beneath these. An interesting and attractive pattern of growth.

COLOR: Crimson pink; also a ruby-red form.
HEIGHT: 3 to 5 feet.
SEASON OF BLOOM: Summer.
LOCATION: Sunny, moist fields, pastures and hillsides; also swamps.
SOIL: Wet sandy soil best.
TRANSPLANTING TIME: September —but little cultivated.
PROPAGATION: Seed; layering.
DON'T PICK.
RANGE: Eastern states and Canada.

SWAMP ROSE, PASTURE ROSE,
CAROLINA ROSE *(Rosa carolina)*.
Rose Family
A beautiful deep-pink single rose with
an abundance of gold stamens at the
center. Fragrant, especially in the warm
noon sun and after a rain. Flowers
are followed by round red fruit that
is highly decorative on the plant. In
some adventurous moment try rose-
petal jam. Blend the petals with honey,
water and lemon juice. Another experiment: Cut up rose petals, mix with
butter and store in the refrigerator a
few days for making exotic and delicious sandwiches.

COLOR: Pink.
HEIGHT: 2 to 7 feet.
SEASON OF BLOOM: Summer.
LOCATION: In open or wooded
areas, both wet and dry.
SOIL: Should be spaded deeply,
with addition of good topsoil, well-
decayed manure and wood ashes or
lime if soil is acid.
TRANSPLANTING TIME: Early
spring or early fall. Good for shrub
borders.
PROPAGATION: Suckers.
FRAGRANT.
MAY PICK.
RANGE: Nova Scotia to Georgia,
west to Minnesota and Texas.

TWINFLOWER, DEER VINE
(Linnaea borealis). Honeysuckle Family
The name *borealis* indicates that this
flower grows in the north. In addition
to being found in North America, it
appears far north around the world,
the American form being somewhat
larger. It flourishes also in some mountain areas southward. A delightful
and charming trailing vine with a
rough woody stem and evergreen
leaves. Nodding bell-shaped flowers
in pairs terminate the stalks. The
flowers are deep pink within, pale pink
without. Makes great patches of
groundcover under young spruces in
the forests of Nova Scotia. *Linnaea*, of
course, is in tribute to Linnaeus.

COLOR: Pale pink to crimson
pink.
HEIGHT: Trailing.
SEASON OF BLOOM: Summer.
LOCATION: Mossy evergreen
forests in deep shade.
SOIL: Acid, peaty.
TRANSPLANTING TIME: Spring or
fall.
PROPAGATION: Runners; it
spreads fast where it grows at all.
Suited only to cool climates.
FRAGRANT. Almond-scented.
MAY PICK.
RANGE: Alaska to Labrador,
south to Nova Scotia and in moun-
tains of Northern United States.

WESTERN BLEEDING-HEART
(*Dicentra formosa*). Fumitory Family
Grows rampantly in Yosemite National Park, Oregon and Washington.
The heart-shaped flowers form in
graceful swirling sprays along the
stems. Gray-green leaves, delicate and
soft to touch, are beautifully cut and
lobed. The Western counterpart of the
Fringed Bleeding-heart.
    COLOR: Pink and rosy purple.
    HEIGHT: 1 to 2 feet.
    SEASON OF BLOOM: Spring, some-
times again in autumn.
    LOCATION: Rich, moist woods.
    SOIL: Acid, well-drained.
    TRANSPLANTING TIME: Fall.
    PROPAGATION: Seed; division; root
cuttings. Best for rock garden. Prefers
light shade; needs shade at midday.
    MAY PICK.
    RANGE: British Columbia to
northern California and Yosemite.

WOOD LILY, RED LILY, PHIL-
ADELPHIA LILY (*Lilium philadel-
phicum*). Lily Family
The most dramatic and exciting Lily
of all. Flowers open upward and petals
are separated. Each bloom stands
rather like a vivid orange-red tulip. But
when you move close you see the
basic Lily shape and also interesting
purple-brown spots on the inner part
of the cup.
    COLOR: Orange-scarlet with
purple-brown spots.

    HEIGHT: 2 to 3 feet.
    SEASON OF BLOOM: June to early
July.
    LOCATION: Found in hemlock-oak
woods, rich, rocky, acid soil and spattered shade. It is really luminous in the
shadows; there are never more than
a few in one place.
    SOIL: Acid. Use sandy loam with
leaf mold.
    TRANSPLANTING TIME: Fall.
    PROPAGATION: Seed; lifting and
dividing bulbs. A Lily that is hardy in
cold climates but difficult to grow.
    DON'T PICK.
    RANGE: Eastern Canada, North-
eastern states, Appalachians.

CARDINAL FLOWER, INDIAN
PINK (*Lobelia cardinalis*). Lobelia
Family
Wherever this plant lifts its slim red
spires of vivid, loosely set blossoms the
hummingbirds gather, especially in
the early morning and at dusk. These
exquisite creatures are the main means
of fertilization as the flower tube is
too long and slim for most insects to
reach into.
    COLOR: Deep but vivid red.
    HEIGHT: 2 to 4 feet.
    SEASON OF BLOOM: Summer and
early fall.
    LOCATION: Low wet areas along
streams, swamps, ditches, at edge of
woods. Needs some shade.
    SOIL: Moist and rich, usually
acid.

TRANSPLANTING TIME: Spring or early fall.

PROPAGATION: Seed. Stalks may be cut back after blooming to produce leafy shoots at base.

DON'T PICK.

RANGE: Eastern half of the United States and southern Canada.

COAST JOINTWEED (*Polygonella articulata*). Buckwheat Family

If you see a misty blur of pink along the beach among the grasses, walk close—it is probably this flower. The tiny bloom is almost too small to see at all without a pocket magnifying glass; but with one you can appreciate an exquisite and appealing form and shape. These tiny specks of beauty cluster up a slim, almost hairlike branching stalk.

COLOR: Dusty pink.

HEIGHT: 4 to 12 inches.

SEASON OF BLOOM: Summer and fall.

LOCATION: Sandy places in full sun or spattered shade.

SOIL: Acid, well-drained.

TRANSPLANTING TIME: An annual; not practical to transplant.

PROPAGATION: Seed.

MAY PICK.

RANGE: Coastal areas, Maine to Florida, and bordering the Great Lakes.

COMMON THISTLE (*Cirsium lanceolatum*). Daisy Family

A common plant and a beauty, but one to respect and approach with care. Best of all to admire from a distance. If you are impervious to sharp spines, the large furry purple blooms make dramatic bouquets. The thistle is an emblem of Scotland. An interesting legend says that the Norse invaders, wading barefoot through the moat to seize Staines Castle at night, found it dry and filled with thistles. Their cries of pain woke the guards and the Norsemen were defeated.

COLOR: Magenta.

HEIGHT: 2 to 4 feet.

SEASON OF BLOOM: Summer and fall.

LOCATION: Widely distributed. Pastures, roadsides.

SOIL: Adaptable.

TRANSPLANTING TIME: Spring.

PROPAGATION: Seed.

MAY PICK.

RANGE: Naturalized across most of Canada and the United States.

DEPTFORD PINK (*Dianthus armeria*). Pink Family
From the midst of small hairy erect leaflike bracts, clusters of tight-together crimson flowers emerge. Petals are jagged-edged and toothed, and blossoms resemble those of Sweet William, but less opulent. Named for the town of Deptford, England; where the plant grows in great drifts and sweeps. It is naturalized here from Europe, where it originally escaped from gardens.
COLOR: Crimson pink.
HEIGHT: 6 to 18 inches.
SEASON OF BLOOM: Summer and fall.
LOCATION: Sunny fields, dry meadows, roadsides.
SOIL: Light, on the dry side, and with some lime.
TRANSPLANTING TIME: An annual; not practical to transplant.
PROPAGATION: Seed.
DO PICK.
RANGE: Eastern states.

SEASON OF BLOOM: Summer and fall.
LOCATION: Low, moist woods, sandy swamps, along streams.
SOIL: Rich, moist.
TRANSPLANTING TIME: Spring.
PROPAGATION: Cuttings. Suitable for a wild garden.
DON'T PICK.
RANGE: Maine to Florida, Ontario to Texas.

CLIMBING HEMPWEED (*Mikania scandens*). Daisy Family
An attractive twining vine that drapes over bushes along moist river banks. Where heart-shaped leaf and stem join the vine, clusters of small downy flowers emerge. Botanical name honors Joseph G. Mikan, a botany professor at Prague University.
COLOR: Flesh-pink disc flowers without rays.
HEIGHT: 5 to 15 feet, climbing.

JOE-PYE WEED, PURPLE BONE-SET (*Eupatorium purpureum*). Daisy Family
Blossom clusters composed of many soft bristly florets of a dusty magenta, a beautiful tone for fall—suggestive of the mountain mists of this season that one sees at dusk over the valleys. Leaves in whorls of six, and stem rough and hollow. The Indians of

New England used this plant in a brew that was said to be a cure for fevers.

COLOR: Dusty magenta.

HEIGHT: 3 to 10 feet.

SEASON OF BLOOM: Early fall.

LOCATION: In low, moist woods and thickets, along streams.

SOIL: Needs rich soil with plenty of moisture.

TRANSPLANTING TIME: Spring or fall.

PROPAGATION: Division; removal of side shoots.

MAY PICK.

RANGE: Southern Canada to Florida, west to Oklahoma and Texas.

LADY'S-THUMB, HEARTWEED (*Polygonum persicaria*). Buckwheat Family

A sprawly, rambling little plant covered with miniature flowers shading from soft pink to purple, in little spikes. Grows in waste places all across the temperate United States. Note that the leaves are interestingly marked with a darker green triangle in the center.

COLOR: Dusty pink to dark purple.

HEIGHT: 1 to 2 feet.

SEASON OF BLOOM: Summer through late fall.

LOCATION: Widespread in waste areas.

SOIL: Adaptable.

TRANSPLANTING TIME: An annual; best grown from seed.

PROPAGATION: Seed; self-sows.

MAY PICK.

RANGE: Throughout the United States and southern Canada, except far North. Naturalized from Europe.

FIELD MILKWORT, PURPLE CANDYROOT (*Polygala viridescens*). Milkwort Family

A leafy branching species with rose-purple blooms resembling those of a small-scale clover. Slim leaves are linear and tapering to a point. Most attractive when arranged in bouquets with a few stalks of Goldenrod and Asters. *Polygala* derives from *poly*, meaning much, and *gala*, milk. This refers to the plant's supposed virtue as a promoter of milk in cows that feed on it. Roots have a wintergreen fragrance when crushed.

COLOR: Magenta-pink, sometimes paler.

HEIGHT: 6 to 12 inches.

SEASON OF BLOOM: Summer and fall.

LOCATION: Damp fields, pastures, salt meadows, but sometimes in drier sandy places.

SOIL: Moderately acid.

TRANSPLANTING TIME: Spring; but best grown from seed as plant is an annual.

PROPAGATION: Seed.

MAY PICK.

RANGE: Nova Scotia to North Carolina and Louisiana.

OSWEGO TEA, BEE BALM
(*Monarda didyma*). Mint Family
A "musical" plant; constantly, during the day, this one is alive with bumblebees and hummingbirds. The stir and hum of both make a constant and pleasant summer sound. Then come the butterflies to bring their color and beauty to the scene. Flourishes in shady woodlands where it stands tall and dignified beside a stream. Note how the leaves immediately below the flower cluster are stained red, almost as if the plant had more color than it could crowd into the blossom and had spilled the leftover on the foliage. The name *didyma*, from the Greek, means "paired" and indicates the way the stamens on each individual flower come in twos. The leaves were used for tea at Oswego, once an outpost on Lake Ontario.

COLOR: Scarlet red.

HEIGHT: 2 feet.

SEASON OF BLOOM: Summer and fall.

LOCATION: In moist woods, along streams, shady woodlands.

SOIL: Acid.

TRANSPLANTING TIME: Early spring.

PROPAGATION: Seed, lifting and dividing clumps.

AROMATIC LEAVES.

MAY PICK.

RANGE: Quebec to Georgia and Tennessee.

PINESAP, BEECHDROPS (*Monotropa hypopithys*). Shinleaf Family
A flower of mystery, of dim shadows, deep woods and private, remote areas far from the hand and life of man. The stiff, waxy urn-shaped flowers themselves seem almost unreal. Thrives under oaks and pines, where it is literally fed and nourished by sap from the surface roots of these trees. A relative of the Indian Pipe.

COLOR: Faintly pink to tawny-reddish; sometimes lemon yellow.

HEIGHT: 4 to 12 inches.

SEASON OF BLOOM: Summer and fall.

LOCATION: In dark and humid woods, under pine or oak trees.

SOIL: Acid.

TRANSPLANTING TIME AND PROPAGATION: Almost impossible to move successfully. The plant is saprophytic, blackens when disturbed. It does spread and self-sow; the seeds are like dust.

VAGUELY FRAGRANT.

DON'T PICK.

RANGE: Eastern North America.

RAGGED ROBIN, CUCKOO FLOWER (*Lychnis flos-cuculi*). Pink Family
A ragged flower, casual, carefree and windblown, brought originally from

Europe. Leaves are slender and ribbon-like. The plant is downy at the bottom, slightly sticky near the top. Lower leaves are blunt-tipped, upper ones pointed. A gypsy plant with much charm and appeal.

COLOR: Pink, crimson, blue or white.

HEIGHT: 1 to 2 feet.

SEASON OF BLOOM: Summer and fall.

LOCATION: In sunny damp fields, pastures, waste places, along streams.

SOIL: Adaptable if soil is moist.

TRANSPLANTING TIME: Spring.

PROPAGATION: Seed; division.

MAY PICK.

RANGE: Eastern United States.

RUGOSA ROSE (Rosa rugosa). Rose Family

Who can say which is more beautiful —the blossom with its crowded gold stamen at the center or the round fat rose hips of autumn? The fragrance of the flowers spreads far and wide, a deep rich scent in the morning, at dusk, in the noon sunlight and after a rain. Walk along the rim of the beach where these grow, and the scent travels with you. The hips make delicious jam and jelly when you strain out the seeds. Both are high in vitamin C.

COLOR: Pink, crimson, white.

HEIGHT: 2 to 6 feet.

SEASON OF BLOOM: Summer and fall.

LOCATION: Seashore areas, along beaches, sandy banks. Will grow far north.

SOIL: Light, sandy.

TRANSPLANTING TIME: Early spring or early fall.

PROPAGATION: Suckers and layering.

FRAGRANT.

DO PICK.

RANGE: To some extent naturalized, or planted and spread, from northeast Asia to eastern United States and Canada, especially near the coast.

SAND VERBENA (Abronia villosa).

Four-o'clock Family

Striking thickish light blue-green leaves stretch and straggle casually over the desert areas of Arizona, California and Utah. Thick stems, sticky and hairy, are pink. The delicate, highly fragrant flowers resemble the garden verbena. A most beautiful plant and flower well worth a pause in the desert to appreciate it.

COLOR: Lilac-pink.

HEIGHT: Creeping.

SEASON OF BLOOM: Summer and fall.

LOCATION: Deserts, mesas.

SOIL: Well-drained sandy loam best.

TRANSPLANTING TIME: Spring.

PROPAGATION: Seed; cuttings from fresh shoots.

VERY FRAGRANT.

DO PICK.

RANGE: See above.

SLENDER GERARDIA (*Gerardia tenuifolia*). Snapdragon Family
The flowers are tiny flaring trumpets and the leaves sharp as a darning needle. Watch out they don't prick you when you pick them. Interestingly, the plant is a hungry one. It derives its nourishment not only from the soil; in addition the roots fasten on the roots of other plants and rob them of food.

COLOR: Magenta.
HEIGHT: 10 to 20 inches.
SEASON OF BLOOM: Summer and fall.
LOCATION: Dry, sunny fields, open woods, meadows, mountainous areas.
SOIL: Neutral.
TRANSPLANTING TIME: An annual; best grown from seed.
PROPAGATION: Seed, but difficult unless in same soil as parent plant.
DO PICK.
RANGE: Quebec to Georgia and west to Texas.

SMALL-LEAVED BURDOCK, COMMON BURDOCK (*Arctium minus*). Daisy Family
A plant that travels far and wide. The hooked burs cling to your clothing when you pass and thus are conveyed great distances to spread the species. Lower leaves are heart-shaped. Flower heads themselves are spiny and somewhat forbidding. Naturalized from Europe.

COLOR: Purple.
HEIGHT: 4 to 6 feet.
SEASON OF BLOOM: Summer and fall.
LOCATION: Sunny fields, gravelly waste areas.
SOIL: Adaptable.
TRANSPLANTING TIME: Spring (only young plants, as older plants have long taproots).
PROPAGATION: Seed.
DON'T PICK.
RANGE: Across North America. Naturalized from Europe.

STEEPLEBUSH, HARDHACK (*Spiraea tomentosa*). Rose Family
A woolly plant whose dark-green leaves are whitish to yellowish and downy beneath, and whose terra-cotta red stems are furry to touch. The steeplelike flower stalks come in great plumes and are composed of myriad minuscule florets in delicious shades of pink. These vary from pale to deep,

depending on the soil the plant grows in. The succession of blooms is not the usual bottom to top, but from the top of the flower stalk *downward*.

COLOR: Pale pink to deep pink.
HEIGHT: 2 to 4 feet.
SEASON OF BLOOM: Summer and early fall.
LOCATION: Moist meadows and swamps, in full sun or semi-shade.
SOIL: Slightly acid.
TRANSPLANTING TIME: Spring or fall.
PROPAGATION: Cuttings.
DO PICK.
RANGE: Eastern half of U.S. and part of southeastern Canada.

ROSE MALLOW, SWAMP ROSE
(Hibiscus moscheutos). Mallow Family
Flowers that may be four to six inches across are borne singly and, though much larger, suggest the Hollyhock in their habit of growth. The swamps on Cape Cod glow with these blooms, and on hot summer days, how cool and refreshing they are in their light-pink tones. The leaves are densely white and woolly beneath. The five-petaled flowers are interestingly veined.

COLOR: Pale pink, white.
HEIGHT: 4 to 8 feet.
SEASON OF BLOOM: August to September.
LOCATION: In sunny marshes and bogs along the eastern coast and throughout the Great Lakes area.
SOIL: Adaptable, but should not be too dry.

TRANSPLANTING TIME: Fall.
PROPAGATION: Seed; division of clumps.
DON'T PICK.
RANGE: Massachusetts to Florida and Missouri.

WOOD SAGE, AMERICAN GERMANDER *(Teucrium canadense)*.
Mint Family
Small lavender flowers are arranged in circles around the stalk toward the top. These open in succession from the bottom up. Note how the lower lip of the bloom is prominent and makes a fine landing spot for bees. The lance-shaped leaves are softly downy beneath. The Latin name honors Teucer, the first king of Troy, because he allegedly used the plant (another species) medicinally. In the Middle Ages it was an herb for "strewing"; it was scattered on floors to refresh the air of chambers and halls.

COLOR: Pale purple, magenta, sometimes cream color.
HEIGHT: 1 to 3 feet.
SEASON OF BLOOM: Summer and fall.
LOCATION: Low, wet woods and thickets, sunny bogs.
SOIL: Should be moist.
TRANSPLANTING TIME: Summer.
PROPAGATION: Seed; cuttings; division. Good for a wild garden.
MAY PICK.
RANGE: Widespread in southern Canada and from Maine to Nebraska and southward.

Part Two

GARDENING
WITH
WILDFLOWERS

Listening to Nature

A human being, as he finds and lives in his right environment in life, usually thrives and is happy and healthy. Likewise a wildflower. When next you walk through woodlands, meadows and along streambanks, take special note of the wildflowers and under what a vast variety of different conditions they grow and flourish. There are those that like shade, those that thrive in sunlight, and those that are at home with water nearby. Success in growing wildflowers on your own place depends largely on being able to provide the conditions under which they will do well. These are secrets nature readily shares with those who have an observant eye.

There are great opportunities today for digging native plants and bringing them home to grow on your own land without breaking conservation laws—in fact, with the blessing of the conservationists. All across the country, developments, new highways, roads, reservoirs and dams are underway. Bulldozers seem to be running rampant these days. We, with our trowels, shovels and baskets, have a glorious chance not only of spreading beauty but at the same time saving plants that would otherwise be destroyed. So we can be a rescue squad while doing ourselves a favor. In almost every community there are areas providing a challenge and opportunity for those who would like to grow native plants.

You need to be observant about where and how each variety you would like to have grows in its native habitat. There are five specific classifications of landscape to differentiate. One, high dry woodland; two, low woodland or brookside; three, dry pasture, meadow or roadside;

four, wet pasture or meadow, ditch or bog; five, fringe of woodlands. In which location do your chosen plants live? And then the all-important question: Have you something comparable at home?

Next to consider is the kind of soil the variety you want grows in. Pick up a handful. Get a good feel of it. Is it clay? Is it rocky? Is it loam? Is it filled with leaf mold? Or is it very sandy? The more nearly you can approximate this earth the more chance of success you will have with whatever you are considering moving.

Now, contemplate the slope of the land. Are the flowers you would like to take home growing on a north, south, east or west slope? A compass will be a help here. The land slope determines how much sun the area will get during the day, how much soil warmth during the year. Plants on a southern slope will have warmer earth around their roots than those growing on a northern slope. They will prefer the same slope in your garden. The tilt of the land also instructs you about drainage. Wildflowers found on a steep hillside will pine away in a boggy site. Those in a gully where there is moisture will languish if you put them on a high dry hillside.

Are the plants you would like growing in half shade, full or both? As you become more aware, you will find there are many different kinds of shade. There is the dense shade of low bushes, the light shade of taller bushes and the open shade of high trees. Deciduous shade is variable, while evergreens provide year-round shadow. All these conditions affect growth.

Certain flowers do best with rocks nearby. Some like the roots of trees as neighbors. Others flourish on the sunny side of a fallen log, or in the lee of a stone wall or stump. When you find plants doing especially well in a certain place take very careful note. Why not carry a small notebook with you and jot down a record as you go along?

Also try to sense the atmosphere of a location. Is your selected variety growing in the windless quiet of a pine woods or on a breezy hillside? Or is it located in the flaming gaiety of a meadow where everything is open and the sun streams down?

When you think in terms of naturalizing wildflowers bear in mind that it is always far easier to go along with *what is*. It is much more satisfactory to *choose plants that suit the soil and location you have* than to consider changing your earth and conditions to suit the variety you would like to grow. If you live in a sunny field, forget about Hepaticas, Indian Pipes, Trout Lilies and Arbutus. If you live in a woods the former will thrive, but don't give a thought to Daisies and Black-eyed Susans.

For ultimate success and a riot of native plants in your own garden, begin in a small and simple way. Proceed slowly. Choose just a few plants that you think will do well. Try these and study their adjustment. Then, branch out and try a few more. While you may want many, many plants, if you start with a small number of the right plants for the right spot they will soon multiply, and you will be saved a great deal of effort. It will not be necessary for you to plant flowers by the hundreds. Nature will do it for you.

Collecting plants from the woods is about one of the most delightful and satisfying occupations there is. Not only is it fun to go wandering with a trowel and a basket, but the flowers you bring home and set out the same day will bring you the atmosphere of the place where you found them—a hint of mountains or far-off meadows or streambanks.

Early spring is a fine time to move a great many wildflowers. It is easy to find and recognize them at this season. The lushness of summer growth is apt to bury them. You can successfully move quite a number when they are about to flower, such as Dutchman's-breeches, Foamflower, Columbine, Hepatica and Bloodroot.

In the early summer when the plants are still six to ten inches high, Black-eyed Susans, Daisies and Goldenrod can be moved. During a rainy week, almost any time during the summer, if you take enough soil with each plant, you can move almost anything. However, general conditions are more favorable if you do it in the spring.

The equipment that you need for digging up plants in the wild includes a few wooden flats or corrugated boxes, some large baskets, newspapers, a shovel, a trowel, pruning shears, large pieces of plastic and a jug of water. You probably won't need all of these for every moving project, but if you keep them in the back of your car you'll be prepared for any emergency, such as coming upon an unexpected building development in process when you are driving about, and perhaps a great hillside of Trillium about to be destroyed.

In digging, take as much soil as you possibly can and disturb the roots as little as possible. Suppose you are going to dig up a Daisy plant in the spring. Clear away the leaves and grasses. Cut around the plant about eight inches in diameter. You may sever a few outside roots, but it won't matter. Cut some of the larger roots with pruning shears if you must. Gently lift out the root ball and wrap the clump in newspaper or a plastic bag, and water it. If you are taking a half-dozen Daisies, dig a bushel basket of soil from the same meadow and they will be thoroughly at home on your own land. Always be sure to bring home a small basket of ground litter, twigs, leaves, grasses, small stones, bark, lichen, moss and whatever else is around the varieties you are moving. This groundcover contains beneficial bacteria important to the plants' development.

How different it is to transplant Partridge Berry. In this case all you need is a pair of scissors. Take some of the long trailing stems that have wisps of root on them. Work them up out of the soil with a trowel. Put them in a plastic bag with some water and wet moss. When you get home, set the plants in the shade while you decide the best place to establish them.

Bear this in mind when you set out wild plants: Keep them close, as close to each other as you found them in woods or field. They are much more effective grown in clumps than a single plant here and another there. Also, move away any surrounding growth, so they will have space in which to stretch.

When planting Daisies, for example—if there are several in the clump you have dug up, leave them together. Set the crown at the same depth you found it growing. Be careful not to set it too deep or too high. Water each clump as soon as planted and put a few bits of grass or leaves over the surface to hold the moisture in.

The Partridge Berry may be cut into six-inch lengths, or even shorter if the pieces have good roots clinging to them. Cover the stems with soil, permitting only the small round leaves to emerge.

Newly set out wildflowers need watering every day until a few heavy rains come along.

If there are no bulldozers operating in your vicinity, no developments being built, consider the many wildflower nurseries throughout the country from which to acquire plants. If there is a nursery near you, try to make an appointment and go when the grower is free and can help you select the varieties *suitable to your land and conditions.*

In consulting with the nurseryman tell him exactly what these are. Have you sun, shade, clay, loam? Try to describe your place in detail, and then be guided by his suggestions as to what will grow. It is all too easy to get carried away with your own and the grower's enthusiasm for the beauty and charm of certain plants; but they will never survive the first transplanting unless their new home is a compatible one.

I have given a lot of details here on transplanting—but as with all gardening there are more than rules to follow. Take whatever I have said and mix it freely with your own observations and hunches. For example, one plant will sometimes grow in more than one kind of location, so let your exploring be broad. Lady's-slippers will grow in an oak grove, but also where there are pines and along stone walls. Daisies thrive along the dry and dusty roadsides as well as in the meadow where it is not so dry. Bee Balm will grow on a streambank in semi-shade; it will also grow in full sun where it is drier. These are a few of the variables to consider. First and foremost, listen to nature, and then to your own experience. Nature and your own awareness together will tell you what you need to know, and the flowers you move will flourish.

Twelve Rules for Success in
Moving and Growing Wildflowers

1. Choose healthy material, either purchased or dug from the wild.

2. Insofar as possible, give each plant the soil in which it grew in its native state, the same location, amount of sun and all similar conditions. Set the plant at the same soil depth at which it grew. Firm the earth around the roots but not so heavily as to smother the plant.

3. Clear a little space around the holes where you dig in new plants and keep cleared until the new wildflowers are established.

4. Water the first few days, or until several hard rains have fallen and you feel the plant has settled in.

5. At first, protect the wildlings from cats and dogs or any intruders who might tramp on them.

6. Set plants in the ground very promptly after they have been dug or purchased—the same day, if possible.

7. Bring plenty of woodland litter to scatter on the ground around newly set plants.

8. Start simply and in a small way, trying a few of a variety to see if they will adapt to your chosen spot.

9. Develop your sixth sense about what certain plants need as you go wandering in wild areas and observe wildflowers in their native states.

10. Mulch the first year or so with dead leaves in winter if the plants are from the woodland, with old grass if they are from a meadow, with whatever might fall on them where they came from.

11. Clear the mulch in the spring, gradually and carefully—never all at once. Always leave some mulch, however, to decompose and feed the plants.

12. Spend time with your wildflowers, walking among them, appreciating them, sensing their needs and whether or not you have the right plant in the right place. If you suspect you have not, move it.

Five Gardens for Different Conditions

Have you a woods, a stream, a stretch of deep shade, or do you live by the sea or near a sunny meadow? Whatever your land situation, there are a large number of wildflowers waiting to grow for you. Know the joy of creating a garden of native plants wherever you are. The care is minimal and the rewards and delights are endless.

A WOODLAND GARDEN

You have been walking in the mountains. Perhaps in deep woods where filtered sunlight pours through to catch a bank of Trillium here and shine on a clump of Columbine there. Just beyond are Ferns, Wood Anemones and a single golden Lady's-slipper. The earth is soft and bouncy underfoot, the air fresh and invigorating. No sound of human voice or of cars, only silence and solitude, an atmosphere of privacy and the loveliness of wildflowers. As you walk along, you feel a deep quiet growing within. Far-reaching thoughts fill you, thoughts you would surely never have walking down the village street.

Why not make a woodland garden on your own place somewhere? You could raise a variety of the same wild plants. You could retire from the press of events and wander along secluded paths. In our busy lives we all need interludes of escape. How replenished we feel after a brief time apart in the world of nature! A small woodland can provide this sense of replenishment as well as the charm of myriad wildflowers.

A woodland garden will flourish almost anywhere there is some shade. Perhaps you have the shady side of a high wall or hedge, an area under a single large deep-rooted tree, a place along the north house wall, a stretch of tall and thick shrubbery that could be pruned and shaped and a path cut through. Have you a few hemlocks, firs, beech or oak? Or pines? If so, you have the ingredients with which to start a woodland garden.

Here are five important conditions for a successful woodland garden:

1. Plenty of shade with some filtered sun.
2. Acid soil.
3. Earth that is loose and friable.
4. Splendid drainage.
5. Wind protection.

Your pattern for a woodland garden, the landscaping and design, is easiest of all to come by. Go wandering through your favorite woods with pad and pencil. Take note of what is growing where, and what particularly appeals to you. Observe how a rock is wedged in with a clump of Bloodroot to one side of it. Notice that mossy north bank with Arbutus spilling down it. Don't overlook the Fringed Gentian and how it grows in a spot where it catches the sun. Here under pines are red-and-yellow Columbine. Half-hidden in the shadows, but where some sun filters through, are several plants of Dutchman's-breeches. Up by those rocks you see the snowy Toothwort. Wake-robin stands in dignity, its nodding red flowers enhancing the scene.

From observing the designs and patterns in nature you will be able to plan and arrange your own. Be sure to have your path curve so you cannot see all of it at once. Let there be surprise vistas and turns. In most woodlands you find an occasional old stump on which you can rest for a few moments. Be sure to have something comparable in your new woodland.

The joy of a woodland garden is that, once it is established, it needs almost no care. Leaves from trees above fall, creating a winter mulch. Oaks and pines provide the desired acidity. Wild plants need no supplementary food. Decomposing leaves produce their supplies of nitrogen, phosphate and potash. Rotting pieces of bark and leaves, small twigs and pine cones, fungi from fallen trees, dried moss and lichen and all sorts of other wonderful items falling among the plants disintegrate and furnish life-giving humus. These also bring an atmosphere of wilderness.

A woodland garden can be large, or it can be rather small. Its charm depends more upon choice of material than upon size. In a small space there is an appealing quality of intimacy. Each individual plant is appreciated. Without too many, each one comes into focus, revealing its special character in detail. So, be it little or large, here in your private sanctuary is your seclusion and your identification with nature.

Some Especially Appropriate Wildflowers to Include in Your Woodland

Bellwort, Bloodroot, Columbine, Common Violet, Dog's-tooth Violet, Dutchman's-breeches (stony but rich soil), False Solomon's-seal, Hepatica, Jack-in-the-pulpit, Jewelweed (wet places), May-apple, Partridge Berry, Pipsissewa, Rattlesnake Plantain, Solomon's-seal, Toothwort, Trailing Arbutus, Wake-robin, Wild Lily-of-the-valley, Yellow Lady's-slipper.

DO YOU HAVE A STREAM?

How lucky you are if a stream wanders through your land, for here along the banks you can have an especially beautiful wildflower garden. A stream garden is a place of constant surprise. Around each turn and bend is something you didn't know was there. The first thing in planning a stream garden is to clear a little path along the edge. The material that wants to be near water can grow on the bank, folding down to the brook. Other varieties can be set on the opposite side of the path.

Such a trail will wind and curve. Even if the stream doesn't wind, be sure the path does. The most interesting and tempting kind of stream garden, like a woodland garden, is one where you are irresistibly drawn along and every few feet discover something new. An area along the water can be planted for a succession of blooms from spring to fall. Among the first to flower is the small Dwarf Iris (*Iris cristata*). This little plant wants a few beams of sunlight, both early in the season, before the leaves are out, and after the leaves drop in the fall. It is charming when it first perks up in the spring and as flowers unfurl from the rich green of the foliage. After the blossoms fade the plant continues to be quite lovely all summer. Deep-green pointed leaves fold over and over each other and bend to fit the contours where they grow, making a beautiful coverlet for the bank of a brook.

Forget-me-nots are another excellent flower for the stream garden. These grow partly in and partly out of water. On the bank several feet above the water level, and in the shade, a cluster of Dutchman's-breeches will flourish. If your brook has a sunny stretch, try the Meadow Parsnip (Golden Alexanders). The soft yellow mist suggests a small version of Queen Anne's Lace, and it soon runs rampant.

Somewhere in the dim shadows set a Jack-in-the-pulpit, or two or three, and a cluster of Yellow Lady's-slippers. Bee Balm thrives near water. A dozen or so of these plants will keep your midsummer musical with the swift whir of hummingbirds. No more exquisite joy exists than watching these ruby-throated creatures poised in mid-air as they dart from blossom to blossom, all the while the sun glinting on their crimson throats. Late in the summer the Cardinal Flower brings a note of vivid red. Perhaps you will have the experience we once had of seeing a scarlet tanager bathing in the shallows at the foot of a cluster of Cardinal Flowers. The filtered sun through leaves above sparkled on both feathers and blooms, and who can say which was brightest?

The beautiful, stately Canada Lily is happiest with feet slightly moist. This flower unfolds in the summer and brings a note of dignity and beauty to your area. Jewelweed is another for the edge of the stream.

To stir your sense of sight and touch and also your sense of smell, plant a little Wild Mint along the stream. It will spread rapidly. Not only can you grow your own mint tea, you can also enjoy the aroma, which is especially strong in the morning, at noon with sun on the plants, at dusk, and always after a rain.

Foamflower, with soft feathery blooms in the spring, along with the snowy flowers of Bloodroot, will enhance your spring walks along the stream border, if they are in a shaded stretch.

From spring to fall something will be happening in the stream garden, something to lure you out along the path. You will want to snip a little here, move a plant there, carve out a special vista somewhere else. Consider what you see as you pause where pause is invited. Perhaps you should remove this branch for a better view, cut that tall grass. Think also in terms of texture. A variety of textures is pleasing to the senses, whether you are consciously aware of it or not. Try to transplant and establish an assortment of mosses. How differently they all feel as well as look! The small Iris provides a contrast to the heart-shaped Foamflower leaves. Meadow Parsnips are soft and feathery, quite unlike the Canada Lily. You want contrast in height as well—some plants that are tall and some that are short.

A plant that is lovely in flower may be equally lovely when not in bloom. We all have a habit of letting our attention be drawn only to flowers and colors. Let's not miss textures and the feel of things, as well as shapes and masses. These all lend as much charm to a garden as color and bloom. Consider the diversified and intricate forms of Ferns.

An old stump lying along the path or a weathered wooden bench issues a provocative invitation. A stream garden is a place to dream, and a place to think and to feel. Let there be spots where you can stop and listen to water rustling past, birds singing or skittering in the leaves. Here you also will smell a great variety of fragrances, including that of the water itself, and here you can watch the flowers grow.

A stream garden is cool and refreshing. A kind of mystery permeates flowing water. As you watch it move past and gently stroke the mossy banks, you wonder where it has come from, this fresh run of water. It had its birth in the depths of the forest in some far-off place, bubbling up, bringing all sorts of deep-down elements that form in the earth's center and gradually work their way up to light and air. Linger where the water slides along and you find yourself wondering where the stream is going. It has come many miles and has many miles to go. And all the while its origins and destiny are a mystery.

Especially Appropriate Wildflowers for a Streambank Garden

Bellwort, Bloodroot, Blue Flag,* Bottle Gentian,* Canada Lily, Cardinal Flower, Common Violet, Crested Dwarf Iris, Dog's-tooth Violet, Dutchman's-breeches, False Solomon's-seal, Foamflower, Meadow Parsnip,* Jack-in-the-pulpit, Jewelweed, Large Flowering Trillium, Marsh Marigold,* Moccasin Flower, Partridge Berry, Pickerelweed,* Showy Orchid, Skunk Cabbage, Spring Beauty, Starflower, Rose Mallow,* Sweet White Violet, Tall Meadow Rue, Toothwort, Virginia Cowslip, Water Hemlock, Wild Blue Phlox, Wild Calla, Wild Lily-of-the-valley, Wild Mint, Wood Anemone.

* *Plants that prefer sun or part sun.*

WILD SEASIDE GARDEN

The wind never stops blowing. Some days it seems to blow everything you want to you and take everything you don't want away. The gulls soar and dip and the sandpipers skitter along in the wash of the waves. Here is a vastness, an openness, a freedom to expand. All this can be reflected in a wild garden at the shore. Colors can be vivid and splashy, flowers packed together, and the whole atmosphere one of abundance and giving.

Against a backdrop of these wide-open spaces and a horizontal landscape, many flowers flourish. Astonishingly, certain ones, including Rugosa Roses, will grow in pure sand. On Cape Cod, Rugosa Roses thrive a few feet from the sea as well as on the banks and bluffs along the shore. Not too far back from the water you find Bearberry carpeting the dunes and spreading spring magic through the beach grass. Impervious to wind and salt spray is the Dusty Miller, another sand-lover, whose lacy gray foliage makes subtle indoor arrangements. The blossoms, like yellow candles, unfold in early summer. Climbing the banks above the water you discern great clusters of Chicory and Bird's-foot Violets. Here, also, perky stems of Scotch Broom and their shiny gold flowers greet the spring, while misty Queen Anne's Lace drifts through summer grasses. And on into the late autumn many different varieties of Goldenrod flourish.

All these plants, and many more, can be transported to grow on your own land and to form the basic pattern of an enchanting seaside garden. In a small area you can have a great variety, many different colors, textures and fragrances. One of the most aromatic of all bushes for the shore is the Bayberry (*Myrica pensylvanica*). Crush a few leaves in your fingers as you pass. The pungency lingers for several minutes. The gray berries, at their best in September, are decorative and charming. Bayberries are a beautiful addition to a seaside garden. You must have staminate and pistillate plants to produce the berries.

An especially lovely flower for the shore is the Beach Pea. The plant rambles and spreads over the ground, sending up delightful deep-purple flowers that open for weeks during the summer and as fall approaches. Silvery down-covered pods develop, which are as attractive as the blooms. A most interesting feature of this plant is the decorative curling tendrils that terminate many leaf stalks.

Black-eyed Susans and Daisies will also flourish at the seashore, along with Buttercups and the Common Milkweed. Somewhere you must have at least one plant of Our Lord's Candle. The great stalk of flowers, which lasts a long time through the summer, can be a real feature of your seaside garden. If you have scrub-pine woods on your place, be sure to plant Blue Lupine. Let Red Clover and Sunflowers roam through your sunny stretches. For a colorful accent, have a few Turk's-cap Lilies. Grow Pearly Everlastings, and you will have the fun of drying them for winter bouquets.

Establishing a seaside garden is a little difficult because of the unusual dryness of the soil at the shore. Right after a rainy spell the wind quickly dries the sandy earth. The preferred time to set out plants or move them to your area is very early spring or late fall. Of course you can have success in a three- or four-day summer rainy spell, but spring or fall is easier.

A seaside garden does not depend on neat beds or edged borders—no wild garden does. Let the flowers grow not in a rigid pattern but in fluent and yielding drifts, with an informal path among them. Let your plan appear as carefree and casual and windblown as the beach itself.

In selecting plants for a seaside garden, be sure to observe the rules for all wild gardens. Duplicate the native conditions as nearly as you can as to soil, sun, slope of land and general atmosphere and environment. For all wild plants, there is a little latitude in conditions under which they flourish, so exercise your careful attention to each plant.

Seaside plants survive the lashing winds and storms because they have amazingly deep roots. The first rule for moving them successfully, therefore, is to dig deep and get all these roots. The second rule is to choose small, young plants. When roots go deep it is much easier to move plants that are small. Young material adjusts more readily.

A third good rule for success in a shore garden is to select as much as possible specimens that stand apart from the parent. As with all transplantings, it is necessary to keep the roots well soaked while plants are being moved and while they are establishing themselves. It is even more important at the seashore, with its drying winds.

A wild garden is an especially appropriate background for a seaside house. It is also easy to manage. With all wildflower gardening there is little to do once you have the plants settled in.

One of the joys of the seashore is collecting shells and bits of driftwood. These can be used to enhance your wild garden. Crushed shells make delightful paths. Driftwood can be used to make benches or merely to lend a decorative note of nature's sculpture to some corner. Bayberry makes a fine background for such pieces.

The seaside garden reflects the expansive openness of the whole seashore scene. It echoes carefree days, dreamy nights with starlight and phosphorescence, and a moon rising from the sea.

Especially Appropriate Plants
for the Seaside Garden

SHRUBS: Bayberry, Beach Plum, Dwarf Blueberry, Rugosa Rose, Sweet Fern.

FLOWERS: Beach Clotbur, Beach Pea, Black-eyed Susan, Bladder Campion, Buttercup, Butterfly Weed, Chicory, Coast Jointweed, Common Milkweed, Common Thistle, Common White Daisy, Daisy Fleabane, Dandelion, Dusty Miller, Goldenrod, Great Mullein, Lupine, Marsh Pink, Marsh Rosemary, Michaelmas Daisy, New England Aster, Our Lord's Candle, Pearly Everlasting, Purple Coneflower, Queen Anne's Lace, Red Clover, Spiked Loosestrife, Sunflower, Rose Mallow, Turk's-cap Lily, Yarrow.

WILDFLOWERS FOR DEEP SHADE

A secluded deep-shade wild garden is a place of subtle light, mysterious shadows, solitude. How cool and refreshing is such a spot on a hot summer day. Here you savor a special quality of quiet. Here you lean against a tree and just stand in contemplation. The nearby Indian Pipes emerge from their bed of pine needles in waxy starkness, Pipsissewa sends up striped leaves in pairs, and from the shadows a Jack-in-the-pulpit beckons.

Many people feel nothing will grow in an area of solid shade. This is not true. If you have good, friable woodland soil you can have a beautiful garden. It is more important in a spot of deep shade, however, to prepare the soil thoroughly ahead of time. Dig down a spade's depth, take out all roots, and incorporate in the top few inches layers of compost, peat moss and woods soil, all of which form life-giving humus.

Quite a number of plants flourish in deep shade; see below for a dozen to choose from. Set out some of each and you will have a garden attractive with some bloom in spring, summer and fall. Among the earliest to flower is Jack-in-the-pulpit. Take a good look at him, and then at his friend, and you will realize that no two are ever alike. They vary in size, color and details of pattern; and this makes them fascinating to grow. Also, they seem to benefit from good garden soil and care, frequently growing taller and larger than in the wild.

The minuscule Partridge Berry blossoms will also charm you early in the spring, along with the waxy-petaled Pipsissewa flowers that, like the leaves, often come in pairs. Rattlesnake Plantain, with interesting leaves, spreads its rosettes to carpet the earth in the shady garden.

Wild Lily-of-the-valley blooms early in the summer, sending up delicate spires from amongst shiny leaves. The May-apple is one of my favorite spring flowers. You must tip up its green umbrella leaves to find the nodding white flowers beneath. Solomon's-seal follows along in its time, swinging gay bells on arching stalks. The foliage of the Blue Cohosh is as appealing as its rather quiet little flowers.

Wintergreen blossoms are like small Lily-of-the-valley blooms and are followed by bright red berries. The plant is attractive at all seasons, not only for blossoms and berries but for the evergreen smooth, glossy foliage and the delicious flavor if you crush and taste a leaf.

Pinesap has flowers that suggest the Indian Pipe. Both these mysterious, ghostly flowers seem hardly to belong on this earth. They are extremely interesting, however, and well worth growing if you have oaks and pines and a well-shaded area.

When life is rushed and days are full, it is with a secret pleasure that you draw aside for a brief time in your deep-shade garden. Here you commune with the surrounding loveliness, sense the presence of nature's spirits. After sitting loose and breathing deep for a few moments, you return to your work refreshed and renewed.

Twelve Wildflowers to Include in a Garden of Deep Shade

Blue Cohosh, Indian Pipe, Jack-in-the-pulpit, May-apple, Partridge Berry, Pinesap, Pipsissewa, Rattlesnake Plantain, Solomon's-seal, Wild Ginger, Wild Lily-of-the-valley, Wintergreen.

A SUNNY MEADOW GARDEN

It is in midsummer that the sunny meadow comes into its own; and the flowers continue on through fall. There is something rather wonderful about a meadow anyway. Perhaps it begins with fragrances. In the morning the grass is wet with dew, and one kind of scent permeates the air. By noon the dew has dried, the sun streams down, bees and butterflies have been busy, and a totally new fragrance fills the air. By dusk the aroma is again different. As long shadows stretch over the grass, a silence fills the meadow that is beautiful to experience as you walk through. A meadow is a place of action. Apart from bees and butterflies, birds are nestling in the tall grass. A small mouse lives in a hole under a Daisy plant. One morning a family of rabbits emerges from a much larger hole to surprise and delight you. Here in the field the praying mantis waits for his prey, and at night the whole area comes alive with fireflies and the sound of summer insects.

In a meadow you can see the wind! Watching the grasses bend and sway you have the illusion of actually seeing the breeze itself.

A meadow can be any size at all. If you haven't a field, and would like one, you have merely to stop mowing a sunny part of your lawn and let it go wild. A meadow can also be formed at the edges of your land.

If you already have a field in which to plant, you are ready for a meadow garden. This is the garden that has to have sun. It can be high or low, wet or dry, but it really must have sun. You must also refrain from mowing until the very end of the summer. This will permit the flowers to go to seed and multiply themselves. If you let your field remain uncut for two or three years, an amazing variety of wildflowers will sprout up from the earth, most of which you never knew were there. To these you can add more plants, and at the same time scatter more seed. Like all wild gardens, a meadow garden involves practically no care or upkeep. It does, however, demand watching each year, to make sure that no wind- or bird-sown young shrubs or trees are getting too large. For nature does not always remain unchanged. A meadow may, in a few years, become studded with young cedar trees, brambles, birches, willows, poplars, what-not. Perhaps you will enjoy this gradual transformation, but if you prefer that beloved meadow, you must uproot most of the unwanted invaders.

The grasses that are mowed should remain on the field. Gradually these decompose, adding humus. Flower stalks, cut down in the fall, shake loose their seeds to spread the species.

Daisies are the original meadow flower, and among the loveliest. Black-eyed Susans come along about the same time. In the low parts where it is a little damp you will find Wood Betony—with the unsentimental alternate name of Lousewort. Don't be discouraged by that name, for the feathery leaf is a delight, like a small green ladder. The flowers also have a casual, carefree look and are most appealing.

A definite must for the meadow garden is Butterfly Weed. This has a deep root and is difficult to transplant, but not impossible. It will flourish in hard, unproductive-looking soil. Among its special charms are the myriad brown butterflies attracted to it during the season. In September (on Long Island) the large and brilliant monarch butterflies visit this plant in large numbers before congregating for their annual flight to the South. You must make an early-morning trip to view the drops of nectar. Each, like a globe of dew or rain, is poised in the center of every blossom, catching the sun and sparkling like an array of diamonds. As butterflies and bees come during the day, this nectar disappears. You could do worse than go out some early midsummer morning and sit for a while contemplating the beauty of the Butterfly Weed. It is one distinguished member of the Milkweed family, all of whose members have a unique and elaborate blossom structure. The seedpods are also attractive when they first form and while they shed their downy seeds, and for a long time afterwards.

The plant of the Butterfly Weed returns year after year, multiplying and growing larger each season. If you sow seeds one fall, you just may have blooms the following year—and you surely will in two years. Butterfly Weed also propagates readily by root cuttings. Set these out in May and by fall you will have a number of fresh young plants.

One of my very favorite of all meadow flowers is Queen Anne's Lace. The blooms, in drifts of white, scatter through the grasses all summer. By fall each head of flowers browns and curls into the most interesting bird's-nest effects. Queen Anne's Lace comes to us from Europe, where it grows about twice as large and tall as here, reaching up waist-high as you walk through a field. An alpine meadow in full bloom is as white as a field of snow. The design of the flower itself, with a radiating umbel of small florets, is well worth observing.

One day you are walking through a meadow, perhaps near trees at the border, and are arrested by a startlingly vivid flower that isn't quite a tulip, but has orange-scarlet petals and stands on a two-foot-high stalk. The segments are narrow at their base, and the upper part often reflexed and almost horizontal. The color is bright as a flame. This is the Wood Lily, and one of our prettiest meadow flowers. It unfolds in June and July and remains in flower for several weeks.

The Daylily is another beauty for your meadow. It was brought long ago from Asia and it escaped to the wild places. Grow this somewhere at the edges of a wilderness area, as the leaves spread and take up a lot of space. While each blossom lasts but a day, every stalk has a great number; this prolongs the blooming period for many weeks. There may be as many as eight or nine buds on every stem. The foliage, arching in a fountainlike manner, is slim as a green ribbon. The plant grows so densely that it crowds out all others, and weeds as well. This is one of the easiest of all to transplant. You can actually slice a clump of roots into several pieces and, if every division has green foliage at the top, plants will take hold and grow.

The Canada Lily is one of our favorite meadow flowers. Lance-shaped leaves grow in tiers around the main stalk. The Lilies are nodding, each on a slender stem. The plant may grow five feet tall; the blooms open in midsummer. They must have drainage, but unlike most Lilies these need a generally wet situation.

Another good meadow plant is the Turk's-cap Lily—the one that does so well at the seashore. This most amiable and adaptable Lily flourishes where it is hot and dry, but also in places with ample moisture. Likewise, in full sun or shade. The startlingly brilliant flower catches the eye from a long distance. It multiplies readily from seed and is a lovely addition to the meadow garden.

One of the most satisfactory of all wild gardens is this meadow area. From the first signs of green in the spring until the last Butterfly Weed fluff has blown away in the fall there is something of interest going on. It is not only the flowers, but also the life, that makes a meadow irresistible—at all seasons, at all times of day.

Especially Appropriate Wildflowers to Include in a Sunny Meadow Garden

Black-eyed Susan, Butter-and-eggs, Butterfly Weed, Canada Lily, Chicory (for late summer), Common White Daisy, Daisy Fleabane,

Daylily, Devil's Paintbrush, Hawkweed, Meadow Buttercup, Our Lord's Candle, Queen Anne's Lace, Red Clover, Spiderwort, Turk's-cap Lily, Wild Geranium, Wood Betony.

Propagate Your Own

When we dream of growing our own wildflowers we seldom consider just a few plants but are more likely to think in terms of dozens. Nature is generous, and we want to be equally lavish when growing wildlings on our own land. A good way of ensuring a large number is to propagate our own. This may be done readily by division of roots, by cuttings or by seed.

A very satisfying way of propagating wildflowers is by division. The best time to do this is early spring when varieties are easy to recognize but have not yet begun to flower. Step one is to prepare the spot where you will set the plants by freeing the immediate area of encroaching roots and other growth and loosening the soil so digging will be easy. Now, in your hand, work the plant roots apart until you have several. Put each one in a hole of its own, leaving it out of the ground as short a time as possible. If there are quite a few, put them in a pan of water to wait their turn to be planted.

In a year or so the new little wildflowers will be, every one, as large as the parent. Different varieties separate differently, but in general this is the procedure. Occasionally you must cut some apart. Be sure to have plenty of roots on each piece. Sometimes you will be separating bulbs or cutting corms.

When the new plants are firmed in the earth, water each one thoroughly. For greatest success with this procedure pick a drizzly, rainy day or a time after a good downpour when the earth is moist. If you are in a dry spell or drought, forget propagating by division until the next showers come.

A second way of propagating wild plants is by means of cuttings. Certain varieties especially lend themselves to this method. A piece of stem is known as a cutting and can be encouraged to form its own separate roots and grow into a plant. You need a small cleared garden spot for doing this. Choose an area of filtered sun. Prepare a small bed by digging and turning over the earth about six inches deep. A good soil mixture to incorporate into the top few inches is well-decayed compost, sand and peat moss in equal parts.

Take four- to six-inch stalks from healthy material. Make the cut clean and sharp and just below a leaf bud or joint. Remove leaves near the base. A number of plants will send out a root from a stem wound; therefore make a slight nick near the bottom of the cutting before dipping it in rooting medium. Rootone, Hormodin and similar products are good mediums. After a dip of the cut end into the medium, insert the stalk a third of its length into prepared earth. We have had success in rooting wildflowers both with and without a rooting medium. While helpful, these are not essential.

Set out the cuttings in rows, each one a few inches from the next; *never let them dry out*. You can also root cuttings in pots of sandy soil. They are actually easier to keep track of this way. Put two or three into a five-inch pot, and when roots have formed move into the garden.

The third way of propagating is by seed—an easy and popular method of acquiring an abundance of plants.

A seed is not only a bit of magic but a miracle. What a pleasure to wander through woodlands and meadows and gather ripening pods just before they scatter their largesse far and wide! Here in the palm of your hand lies a potential hillside of glorious flowers or a meadow of dazzling color and scent.

Growing wildflowers from seed is also a way of acquiring those that are on the forbidden list—those not to be picked or dug. You can always collect a handful of seeds as you walk through woods and fields. Removing pods never harms the plant. The fact that a particular variety is on the conservation list makes it an even more satisfying adventure.

Wherever you go wandering in summer and fall, tuck in your pocket a few envelopes for gathering whatever is ripening. Always keep a stack of envelopes in your car. As you fill them, seal and label them. If the pods are not quite mature, spread them out in the sun at home until they are dry and crisp and the seeds shake out. If possible, plant them the same season, in fact, as soon as you can after harvesting. Wildflower seeds germinate most successfully if sown in earth taken from their native heath. Also woods soil is rich and black and crumbly and a joy to work with. The season for gathering wildflower seed begins in the spring after the early-blooming plants finish flowering, and runs through the whole summer into late fall. You can always find something that has gone to seed to take home.

If you can't sow seeds immediately, store them in a cool, dry place until you can. You may even want to keep fall-gathered ones until the following spring. If unable to get woods soil when collecting, sow seed in equal parts leaf mold, garden loam, sand and peat. Scatter the seed in three-inch-deep flats, in a coldframe, a greenhouse or open ground. For most varieties semi-shade is best. Remember, if you can, the amount of sun and shade in which the parent plant was growing when you gathered the seed, and provide as nearly as you are able a similar situation. Planting in open ground is less demanding but a little perilous, too, for a number of birds and small creatures relish these seeds.

Seeds sown in flats or pots must be kept moist but never soggy. In open ground they are more independent. But these, too, need water in a dry spell.

To create a successful bed, turn over the soil down to a spade's depth. Remove rocks and roots. Replace the top few inches with woodland soil or the mix mentioned above. Let the earth settle a week or so before planting. Be sure to label each variety. Scatter in rows to aid in identifying young seedlings when they come up.

The smallest seeds can be spread on top of the earth with a dusting of fine soil over them. Plant the larger ones a half to a quarter of an inch deep. Some sprout quickly, some seem to take forever. When the first ones are up two inches, separate them to stand three or four inches apart. When they are six or eight inches tall, move them to their permanent homes. Certain seeds need a winter of snow before sprouting; some appear in a week or two. You'll be surprised one way or another once you begin raising wildflowers. An added bonus for your new plants—as we said before—all the little twigs and old leaves that were scattered on the ground where the plants grew are invaluable. Bring home this litter to spread around the seedlings now as they grow.

Another interesting way of sowing wildflower seeds is in some cases the most successful. Scatter seed where you wish the plants to grow and let nature take its course. Do this with Wild Columbine and in a year or two you will have great sweeps of bloom. Other varieties that respond to this treatment are Sunflowers, Daisies, Lupine, Milkweed, Asters and, as we all know, Dandelions.

For success in raising wildflowers from seed keep the bed free from weeds. Cover with leaves and branches in winter. When you set out young seedlings in their permanent place, remove grass roots and encroaching growth. Keep them free from smothering neighbor plants for the first year or two. Then they can hold their own.

While sowing seed you will discover much beauty you had hitherto missed—beauty in the shape, form and texture of the seeds themselves and in their endless variety. Study the most appealing with a magnifier to better appreciate them before you bury them in the ground.

Seeds are fascinating, and those of wildflowers especially so. Not only fascinating but mysterious and incredible. Who can believe that the brown dust from the pink Lady's-slipper pod contains the wealth of beauty that emerges? Did you ever consider how neatly the seeds of the Violet are tucked into their three-parted sheaths as into little boats? The Milkweed seeds burst from their pods and in pure magic toss their fluff into the sunny air, each bit of down bearing a brown waferlike speck of life to a new home.

Part of the miracle is studying one small seed and realizing that here, safely encased and protected yet ready to grow, is the very essence of life itself. Not only is life here in this minute speck but enough nourishment to see it sprouted and on the way. This scrap of magic, this miracle of nature, is a part of yesterday and a promise of tomorrow. And we, in planting and gardening with wildflowers, become an important link with both the past and the future.

NOTE: The caption under each plant listed in Part I indicates the best way (or ways) to propagate that particular plant.

Part Three

WILDFLOWERS
FOREVER

Bouquets of Wildflowers

A bouquet of wildflowers anywhere in your house brings a special atmosphere and a sense of life to the area where it stands.

You can explore the world of drying wildflowers and discover the fun and satisfaction in making your own place mats, winter bouquets, decorated notepaper and other interesting things.

Learn about the great adventure that is going on throughout this country of spreading wildflower beauty along the highways.

What joy and pleasure are involved in picking wildflowers and arranging a variety of bouquets! Once you become interested in native varieties you may want to begin a collection of tiny vases (which can become a fascinating sideline). The spring blooms are the shy ones, and often small. But some midsummer flowers also are quite small. Two or three home grown Pipsissewa blossoms in a miniature container have great charm. And Twinflowers on their delicate forked stems can be enchanting—if you are lucky enough to have them—in a simple measuring glass or short-stemmed wineglass. Violets are appealing in a little vase—Forget-me-nots and Clover, too. All these suggest diminutive arrangements. How many different places there are where you can put small bunches of flowers—the kitchen windowsill, bathrooms, your desk, dresser, end tables and porch.

A pleasant way of entertaining dinner company is to put a little vase of flowers on the table at each place—and let every arrangement be different.

All through the growing season you can have some wildflowers in your house gathered from your wanderings through the countryside and from your own wild garden. Try various combinations and experiment to see what blends with what. An early-summer bouquet of great appeal is a mixture of Daisies, Clover, Wild Roses, Daisy Fleabane and Buttercups. You might combine Robin's-plantain with Violets and Clover also. Bluets are best by themselves in the tiniest vase you have. Honeysuckle is lovely for the fragrance it imparts to your house and is attractive arranged with Daisy Fleabane. Try floating Milkweed blossoms in a low bowl. Blue Flag mixes happily with Scotch Broom and Daisies. Clematis floats gracefully in a low bowl, held out of the water by its own foliage. Yarrow with Black-eyed Susans is a beautiful mixture, and a few Bladder Campions further enhance this bouquet. One of my favorite summer combinations is Daisies, Queen Anne's Lace, Black-eyed Susans and Buttercups. Late in the summer when the meadow flowers are fully out, large splashing bouquets for a tall vase or crock outside the front door could include Black-eyed Susans and Daisies. Branches of Bayberry, where it grows abundantly, can be used in this way, and are also refreshing in warm weather in the fireplace or on the hearth. The dark-green foliage keeps for many days and the woody stems stand erect. In the fall, Goldenrod, Joe-pye Weed and Asters are an attractive threesome by the front door to greet your guests.

Apart from bouquets, it is just plain fun to pick flowers. Queen Victoria used to wear blossoms in her hair. Why not, when out walking, pick a few blooms for your buttonhole or your hair? No flower is too small and insignificant to consider. Be sure to keep a magnifier in your pocket for especially appreciating the tiniest wildflowers. When you are driving, travel with a pail of water in the car. You never know when you want to pause by the roadside to gather an armful of blossoms to take home. (Be sure to observe the rules of which flowers to pick unless they are homegrown in which case you may pick anything.)

These are just a few suggestions to inspire you to take off on your own. The field is broad and vast, and may you have a lovely time picking and arranging.

Some Suggested Flowers
for Especially Appealing Bouquets

SHORT AND MEDIUM	TALL	
Bluets	Asters	Iris
Butter-and-eggs	Beardtongue	Jewelweed
Clematis	Bellflower	Joe-pye Weed
Clovers	Black-eyed Susans	Larkspur
Deptford Pink	Bladder Campion	Michaelmas Daisy
Forget-me-not	Blue Flag	Penstemon
Harebell	Buttercup	Queen Anne's Lace
Lotus	Carolina Rose	Scotch Broom
Milkweed	Common White Daisy	Sego Lily
Pipsissewa	Daisy Fleabane	Shasta Daisy
Robin's-plantain	Datura	Spiderwort
Rugosa Rose	Daylily	Sunflower (dwarf)
Self-heal	Evening Primrose	Water Hemlock
Violets	Goldenrod	Wild Bergamot
Virginia Bluebell	Honeysuckles	Yarrow
Wood Betony		

Out of the past comes a charming old-fashioned custom of sending people flowers that bear a special message. According to old-time lore, a bouquet of Goldenrod sends words of encouragement. Four-leaf Clovers say "Good luck!" A dwarf Sunflower tells the recipient he (or she) is adored. Clematis indicates that the recipient has a high and fine mentality. Have the fun of arranging some of your own combinations from the list below.

SPRING
　　Dandelion—*Oracle*
　　Forget-me-not—*True love*
　　Iris—*Greetings! I am thinking of you*
　　Spiderwort—*Esteem, not love*
　　Violet, blue—*Faithfulness*
　　Violet, sweet—*Modesty*
　　Violet, Yellow—*Rural happiness*

SUMMER
  Carolina Rose—*Love is dangerous*
  Clematis—*Mental keenness*
  Clover, Four-leaf—*Good luck*
  Clover, Red—*Industry*
  Daylily—*Coquetry*
  Evening Primrose—*Inconstancy*
  Larkspur—*Lightness, levity*
  Lotus—*Eloquence*
  Mint—*Virtue*
  Penstemon—*Pleasure without alloy*
  Sunflower, Dwarf—*Adoration*
  White Daisy—*Innocence*

FALL
  Goldenrod—*Precaution, encouragement*
  Michaelmas Daisy—*Afterthought, remembrance*

Adventuring with Dried Wildflowers

When the last wildflower of autumn succumbs to frost and winter begins in earnest, we need not miss these beauties of field and stream and woodland. There is a way of enjoying wildflowers every month of the year—in fact, there are several ways. Just as the historic buildings in Williamsburg, Virginia, are aglow all winter with dried bouquets, the same beauty can be created in our own homes with bouquets of dried wildflowers. The potential is endless for drying and using native plants. Another way of enjoying wildflowers the year around involves the ancient art of Japanese Oshibana (the art of using pressed flowers, dried leaves and plants). These procedures are simple for anyone to follow. A friend once made me some of the most beautiful place mats with pressed wildflowers. This same friend often sends notes to people on writing paper with small native blossoms, dried and pressed, applied to one or two corners.

How do you dry flowers? There is a choice of methods. The simplest is to press the blossoms selected between sheets of newspaper placed under a pile of books for several weeks. You can also lay them between newspapers under the rug in a hallway or wherever you frequently walk. If flowers are somewhat fleshy it is helpful to put them between sheets of Kleenex or paper towels but this is not essential. Perhaps you have had the same nostalgic experience as I had of coming across a pressed wildflower when looking through a book from your shelves. Today there are more sophisticated ways of drying flowers than putting them in a book, but there is still nothing wrong with this easiest method of all.

For blossoms to be used in dried bouquets, air-drying is suggested.

This is a matter of hanging flowers in bunches upside down just after they are picked. The length of time for hanging varies. Each variety goes through different stages of limpness. When the stems snap and the petals are stiff to touch, the material is ready. This may be ten days, more or less. However, it is necessary to leave the flowers hanging until fall. And don't take them down until you are ready to use them. All too quickly they will reabsorb the summer moisture and become limp again. The time to begin arranging dried bouquets is when the house heat is turned on in autumn. Only then can you be sure they will hold their stiffness and shape. Flowers that have a lot of water content are more difficult to dry and the result is less successful.

When you are thinking in terms of dried bouquets, be sure to gather some grasses and weeds and a few cattails, if there are some in your area. These may be dried standing up in a container without water. They will take natural graceful shapes and greatly enhance the bouquets.

Flowers that adapt best to air-drying are those that do not easily wilt. The procedure is as follows:

1. Pick the flowers in full sun on a dry day when they are in peak condition.

2. Choose material that is healthy and free from pests and diseases.

3. Remove all foliage from the stems. This speeds the drying process.

4. Gather the stems together into small bunches secured with a rubber band and suspend head down on wire coat hangers or on nails against the wall.

5. For a drying area, choose a place that is warm, dark and dry, but also airy—perhaps a cellar, a closet or an attic. If you use coat hangers you can suspend them from wires or a rack.

6. Many dried seedpods are as interesting as flowers, so be sure to select some of these to dry by the same method and mix in with the blossoms in arrangements.

A second way of drying flowers is by using silica gel. This chemical powder absorbs moisture so well that flowers buried in it and left for a few days emerge dry, maintaining their original colors and form. The drying time is greatly shortened by use of this medium. However, the blossoms do shrink a bit. A nice large head of Queen Anne's Lace will lose a quarter to a third of its size.

Five pounds of silica gel will dry a great number of wildflowers during the summer. The granular mixture goes under various trade names, such as Flower-Dry or Flora-Cure. These mediums can be purchased at most plant centers. Flowers dried with silica gel are bright and true in color. It takes a week or less for most flowers to dry.

The powder has blue crystals in it; when these turn pink, the powder needs drying out. Spread in a flat pan and leave in a 250-degree oven until the crystals turn blue again. Then it is ready to be used once more. Keep silica gel in a tightly sealed container when not in use. It is harmless to touch and may be handled freely.

When you dry flowers with silica gel, it is helpful to have on hand a large tray, scissors, a sharp knife, some florist's wire and tape, wire cutters, a toothpick, an artist's brush, tweezers. You will also need a variety of sealable containers to fit the flower sizes—perhaps an assortment of cake tins, tin boxes with tight covers and plastic trays. For best results put the flowers in silica gel as soon as gathered. Cut them at their peak, but never when they are wet with rain or a heavy dew. Pick only as many as you can process immediately. Except for varieties with blossoms all the way up the stalk, remove the stem an inch below the bloom. Use your judgment as to how to lay the flowers in place. Each can be set on its side on a bed of silica gel or stood on its head. Refer to the helpful directions that accompany a package of silica gel. Let the bed be about one inch deep to begin with. Sift more silica gel in around the petals until each blossom is completely covered. A soft brush helps cover the petals and blossom head. A toothpick is also an aid in working the powder in between flower parts. Dry several at a time of the same kind of flower and the same general size. Cover the entire bloom with silica gel. Several layers of flowers may be placed in one container. Seal the container with masking tape at the edge of the lid. The average drying time is seven days or less—rarely more than a week. Gently lift out one blossom to see if it is ready before taking all out.

Another and less expensive mix for drying flowers is three parts borax and one part clean, fine sifted sand. The sand may be found in hobby shops or toy departments; it is the variety used for children's sandboxes—never beach sand. I have had very good results with silica gel, but the borax mix is also excellent—so don't worry if you can't find the gel. The borax is used in exactly the same way—the difference is that the drying takes about ten to fourteen days. It has one advantage over silica gel—you can use any cardboard box, and it is not necessary to seal it tight.

When ready to arrange dried flowers into bouquets you must build on new stems. Take an appropriate length of florist's wire and insert it through the one inch remaining of real stem up into the blossom center. Bend the wire and draw it back a little to hold secure. Wrap the wire with green florist's tape. When each flower has a new stalk you are ready to begin.

Different flowers respond to different drying methods. Certain flowers will even dry successfully when stood upright in a vase without water and left for several days. This, of course, is very simple. Refer to the lists on pages 146–147 to find the tried-and-true way for drying the individual varieties you choose to work with. But never hesitate to do a little experimenting on your own. Flowers often may be dried in several ways.

How to Make Place Mats Using Pressed Wildflowers

Buy some plain white or natural-color place mats of smooth plastic. Plain solid-colored mats are also appropriate if you prefer them. They should be free from ridges and designs. Arrange pressed flowers and grasses on a mat in a pattern that appeals to you.

Cut a piece of clear Contact an inch larger than the mat. Place it on a flat surface, sticky side up and exposed. Now here is where skill and patience come in. The arrangement you have so painstakingly made on the mat needs to be transferred carefully, piece by piece, onto the Contact. Here, tweezers help. Since once a flower is set down it cannot be moved, do a little careful thinking and planning before you begin. Continue arranging until you have your complete design *backwards* on the Contact. Now, take the place mat and, beginning at one end, roll it gently and carefully over the pressed flowers spread on the Contact. Fold the extra Contact at the edge over the underside of the mat to make a neat border. Now, turn the mat right side up to see how well you have done. Some of the grasses and flowers may have slipped a little —but with practice your skill develops. The process is a challenge at first, and you might do well to have an extra mat to practice on before doing your final one. If you feel reckless and experimental, you can do your final arrangement on the mat itself and roll the Contact over it. This is a little difficult, as air bubbles are apt to form beneath the Contact. Sometimes these form anyway. However, they may be rolled out with a rolling pin. Use a very simple design for your first set. These make attractive and welcome gifts for any occasion.

Notepaper with Pressed Wildflowers

Sheets of Japanese rice paper, available in craft-supply stores, make this easy—and fun. Mix one part Elmer's Glue to three parts water. Arrange some of your pressed wildflowers—one or two simple, small ones—in the corner of some plain notepaper. Tear a piece of rice paper a little larger than the flower and cover it. With a flat brush, brush the glue over the rice paper; do so gently to prevent tearing. Allow this to dry, and you are ready to write a very special note to a very special friend.

Other Uses for Pressed Flowers

With Elmer's Glue and rice paper, you can attach wildflowers to glass doors to prevent people from bumping their heads. (Clear Contact may also be used.)

Pressed wildflowers can also be fixed on plain lampshades to enhance them. Use your own imagination to think up other ways to use these beauties of the wild.

Flat ceramic plaques may be decorated with arrangements of dried wildflowers and hung against the wall. Sometimes such plaques have places in which to put the flower stems. If they don't, you may attach the stems with wire and Scotch tape.

Nine Hints for Greater Success in Using Dried Wildflowers

1. Fragile, fine flowers press beautifully. Delicate foliage also presses well and is attractive combined with the flowers.

2. Ferns press successfully between newspapers under a rug.

3. Maidenhair Fern dries when placed upside down in sand and borax.

4. Clear plastic spray on especially delicate flowers helps keep the moisture out after they have been dried.

5. Duco cement and fingernail polish used fifty-fifty and dropped (with a medicine dropper) into a flower heart helps hold it together.

6. Thick, heavy flowers, such as Bee Balm and Daylilies, may take longer to dry than others.

7. If petals fall from your most cherished bloom when dry, glue them back with Duco.

8. When you remove the flowers from silica gel or borax and sand, use a fine brush to dislodge any powder or sand that sticks.

9. Goldenrod dries by hanging, but sometimes loses its shape. To restore its original form, hold the blossom head briefly over the steam from a tea kettle. After this you will be able to reshape it any way you wish.

Plants That Dry Well When Pressed

Artemisia (dry foliage too)
Beardtongue, Penstemon
Bellflower
Bladder Campion, White Vein
Blue Curls, Bastard Pennyroyal
Bluets, Quaker-ladies, Innocence
Bush Honeysuckle
Coast Jointweed
Common Violet
False Dragonhead, Lion's-heart
Forget-me-not
Goldenrod
Harebell, Bluebell

Lady's-thumb, Heartweed
Larkspur
Maiden Pink
Marsh Rosemary, Sea Lavender
Michaelmas Daisy
Queen Anne's Lace, Wild Carrot
Scotch Broom
Slender Gerardia
Sweet-scented Bedstraw
Sweet White Violet
Tall Meadow Rue
Twinflower, Deer Vine
Wild Pink

Plants That Dry Well When Hung

Goldenrod
Pearly Everlasting, Moonshine

Seaside Goldenrod
Yarrow, Milfoil

Plants That Dry Well in Sand-and-Borax Mixture or Silica Gel

American Lotus, Sacred Bean
Artemisia (dry foliage too)
Beardtongue, Penstemon
Bellflower
Black-eyed Susan, Coneflower
Blue Curls, Bastard Pennyroyal
Buttonbush, Bushglobe Flower
Chicory, Succory
Common Thistle
Common Violet
Crested Dwarf Iris
Culver's Root
Daisy Fleabane
Daylily
Evening Primrose
False Dragonhead, Lion's-heart
Field Chickweed
Fireweed, Spiked Willow-herb
Forget-me-not
Goldenrod
Harebell, Bluebell
Ironweed
Joe-pye Weed
Lady's-Thumb, Heartweed
Lance-leaved Goldenrod
Large Blue Flag
Larkspur

Lizard-Tail
Meadowsweet
Oswego Tea, Bee Balm
Oxeye-Daisy, Common White
    Daisy
Poor-Robin's-plantain, Rattle-
    snake Weed
Purple Coneflower
Queen Anne's Lace, Wild Carrot
Rabbit-foot Clover
Red Baneberry
Red Clover
Rugosa Rose
Sand Verbena
Scotch Broom
Seaside Goldenrod
Slender Gerardia
Spiked Lobelia
Spiked Loosestrife
Steeplebush, Hardhack
Sweet White Violet
Virgin's-bower, Clematis
Water Hemlock, Spotted
    Cowbane
Western Bleeding-heart
White Thoroughwort
Wild Bergamot

Operation Wildflower

Throughout our country there is a great and stirring move afoot called Operation Wildflower. The general idea is to promote the propagation and growth of wildflowers along the highways of our country. It is a cooperative program of the National Council of State Garden Clubs, the state highway administrations and the Federal Highway Administration. This particular highway-beautification program has a twofold purpose. It not only adds greatly to the scenic beauty of the land but cuts down on the costs of mowing along the roadsides in areas where wildflowers have taken over. In states where the program has been going on for several years, road maintenance costs have been reduced, thus conserving both fuel and labor. Here beauty is paying its own way.

The initial impetus toward spreading wildflowers along our highways came from garden clubs and Highway Department officials. The program is entirely voluntary, some states being more active than others. Federal funds are available for paying the cost of planting the material, but the garden clubs are working together to supply seeds. Individuals in the clubs are collecting seed for planting by local county officials. Even boy and girl scouts are enthusiastically taking part in these activities.

It all began in Texas over forty years ago. Countless varieties of flowers, including Bluebonnets, Gaillardia, Buttercups, the wild Passion Flower, Red Clover, white Poppies, Indian Paintbrushes and Sunflowers, grace the borders of Texas highways. The drama and spectacular beauty is unbelievable as you drive through mile after mile of Bluebonnets reaching to the horizon. Soon the sea of blue merges into delicate Evening Primroses, and a few miles beyond stand acres of Indian Paintbrush. The very air itself seems tinted with these brilliant flowers.

In Texas the carrying out of this project has been directed toward helping nature rather than to a large-scale planting of seeds. Mowing is delayed each year until pods of the various wildflowers ripen and the seeds fall, thus reseeding the roadside for next year's season. In some cases seeds have been harvested or plants gathered to transplant wildflowers from one area to another. This was not a crash program; it has been done over a long period of years.

The biggest job of Texas Highway Department officials was to convince highway engineers that beauty could be practical. They tried to make every engineer and every county foreman, and a number of other people as well, landscape-conscious. In recent years the wife of former President Lyndon Johnson has taken an active interest in the Texas highway beautification program. Maintenance foremen carry pockets full of flower seed, Johnny Appleseed style, particularly Bluebonnets, the Texas state flower, to broadcast along the highways, and they compete annually for the big prize money given by fellow Texan Lady Bird Johnson for the best effort.

This whole plan, originating in Texas, proved so successful that the Federal Government became interested and cooperative, and in 1973 authorized the use of Federal funds to spur other states into action.

The state of Georgia caught the enthusiasm of Texas for spreading wildflowers along the highways. Mrs. Lyndon Johnson helped by sharing the methods and techniques used in Texas with the Highway Department of Georgia. They had to begin from scratch, and the Georgia men needed to learn not only the wildflowers but where the stands were and how to preserve and increase them. The interest and response of the Georgia officials was prompt.

In one instance a slope that had to be graded contained a beautiful stand of shallow-rooted Bird's-foot Violet. Before grading, the men in the Highway Department removed the Violets in blocks of sodlike grass, stacked them in the shade and watered them. Next they removed the topsoil, graded the slope, scratched up the hard earth, replaced the topsoil and the blocks of Violets, watering in. This was very successful.

In addition to Bird's-foot Violets, a few of the flowers most adaptable in this area to highway planting are Black-eyed Susans,

Coreopsis, Primroses, Verbena, Queen Anne's Lace, Butterfly Weed, Angelica, Bachelor Buttons, Goldenrod and Asters.

In Oklahoma the combined efforts of the Highway Department and garden clubs are beautifying twelve thousand miles of highways. A large number of roadsides already had natural stands of wildflowers. The goal is to create many more.

The garden clubs in Oklahoma are working together collecting or buying, and then donating, wildflower seeds to the Highway Department for planting. All are cooperating as well in selecting sites and choosing flowers. Planting locations are marked so that they will be protected, and mowing here is also delayed until the flowers have bloomed and gone to seed. A group of horticulturists and expert hobbyists from around the state have established guidelines for sowing and harvesting. These people have pooled their special knowledge of plant-growth characteristics, when and where to sow seeds, and the amount of seed required. It is interesting to note that they have chosen only wildflowers that are compatible with nearby livestock and cultivated fields.

This program has stirred up a great deal of enthusiasm throughout the state. Nearly a hundred garden clubs have participated, and highways leading to fifty cities have been planted. In Tulsa County alone, hundreds of acres have been beautified by clubs and councils. The varieties thriving include Red Clover, Blue Flax, Verbena, Coreopsis, Purple Vetch, Rudbeckia and Gaillardia. Plans are afoot for also spreading Indian Paintbrush, Evening Primrose, Beardtongue and a number of others. Here, also, it is not only organizations and garden clubs that are working on this project, but individual citizens have joined partnership with those in authority to create roadside vistas of dancing wildflowers in all colors. Anyone driving through the state of Oklahoma will surely be impressed by their beauty, which increases each season.

In Maryland, under this program, garden clubs supply wildflower seeds, bulbs and other propagative material to the State Highway Department, which plants areas mutually agreed upon. The Maryland state flower, Black-eyed Susan, has been seeded on an experimental basis. It spreads readily and, although a biennial, is long-lasting, and given the opportunity soon takes over the area where it was originally set out. In this state there have also been successful plantings of Evening Primrose, Perennial Pea and Flatpea. The Soil Conservation Service and National Plant Materials Center of the U. S. Department of Agriculture are evaluating and experimenting with several other flower species to determine their adaptability for Maryland highways as well as elsewhere.

In South Carolina, Operation Wildflower is also underway. The garden clubs are cooperating with the Highway Department to encourage the existing flora and add new varieties to make the highways more attractive. Among the flowers chosen here are Bachelor Buttons, Coreopsis, Maltese Cross, Chinese Forget-me-nots and Ageratum.

Information and suggestions were sent out for cooperative action by garden club representatives and resident maintenance engineers in each of the forty-six counties of South Carolina. Since this operation was started, the flowers have spread and multiplied. New varieties have taken hold and the highways grow more spectacular each year.

What a wonderful thing it is to realize that all over this country organizations and individuals are cooperating and moving in unison to enhance our highways and beautify the landscape. As the years go on the flowers will multiply and the countryside will become increasingly lovely.

Spring is the great wildflower season—so most people think. But actually, summer and autumn bring just as many blossoms to fields and meadows along our roadsides. At any season it will be an increasing pleasure and satisfaction to drive through the country and realize what can happen when government and individuals work in cooperation.

Wildflowers to Protect

If you are in doubt about picking certain native plants, do check with your garden club or your state conservation officials. A number of wildflowers need our protection wherever we find them. Here is a sample list.

American Brooklime, Speedwell
Atamasco Lily, Zephyr Lily
Beach Clotbur
Beach Pea, Seaside Pea
Bearberry
Bellwort
Bird's-foot Violet
Bloodroot
Blue Cohosh
Blue-eyed Grass
Blunt-leaved Milkweed
Bottle Gentian, Closed Gentian
Bunchberry
Butterfly Weed, Pleurisy Root
California Poppy
Canada Lily, Yellow Meadow Lily
Cardinal Flower, Indian Pink
Climbing Hempweed
Climbing Wild Cucumber, Wild Balsam-apple

Common Thistle
Dog's-tooth Violet, Trout Lily
Dragon's-mouth, Swamp Pink
Dutchman's-breeches
False Solomon's-seal
Five-finger, Cinquefoil
Flaming Sword, Ocotillo
Foamflower, Miterwort
Fringed Gentian
Goldthread
Great Lobelia
Heartleaf Twayblade
Hedge Bindweed
Hepatica, Liverleaf
Indian Pipe
Indian Poke, False or American White Hellebore
Jack-in-the-pulpit, Indian Turnip
Jacob's-ladder
Large-flowering Trillium
Large Purple Fringed Orchis

Leatherleaf Clematis
Marsh Marigold, Cowslip
Marsh Trefoil, Buckbean
May-apple, Wild Mandrake
Moccasin Flower, Pink Lady's-
  slipper
Moss Pink
Nightshade
Our Lord's Candle
Partridge Pea
Partridge Berry, Twin-berry
Pasqueflower
Pinesap, Beechdrops
Pipsissewa, Prince's Pine
Purple Pitcher Plant, Side-Saddle
  Flower
Rattlesnake Plantain
Rose Mallow, Swamp Rose
Rough-fruited Cinquefoil
Round-leaved Sundew
Sheep Laurel, Lambkill
Showy Orchid
Slender Ladies'-tresses
Small Yellow Lady's-slipper
Small-leaved Burdock, Common
  Burdock

Solomon's-seal
Spring Beauty
Starflower
Star Grass
Thimbleweed, Tall Anemone
Toothwort, Crinkle-Root
Trailing Arbutus, Mayflower
Turk's-cap Lily
Turtlehead
Virginia Cowslip, Virginia
  Bluebells
Wake-Robin, Purple Trillium
Western Evening Primrose
White Water Lily
Wild Calla, Water Arum
Wild Columbine
Wild Geranium, Cranesbill
Wild Ginger, Monkey Jugs
Wild Lily-of-the-valley
Wild Lupine
Wintergreen, Checkerberry
Wood Anemone, Windflower
Wood Lily, Philadelphia Lily
Wood Sorrel
Yellow Mountain Saxifrage
Yellow Pond Lily, Spatterdock

Retail Dealers
in Native Plants and Seeds

United States

Brimfield Gardens Nursery, 245 Brimfield Road, Wethersfield, Conn. 06109.
  Catalogue 25¢
Claude A. Barr, Prairie Gem Ranch, Smithwick, S.D. 57782.
Clyde Robin, P.O. Box 2855, Castro Valley, Calif. 94546. Catalogue $1.00
Conley's Garden Center, Boothbay Harbor, Me. 04538. Catalogue 35¢
Dutch Mountain Nursery, Route 1, Box 67, Augusta, Mich. 49012. (Plants
  for birds and conservation)
Edelweiss Gardens, Box 66, Robbinsville, N.J. 08691. Catalogue 25¢
Eugene Mincemoyer, Route 5, Box 329, Jackson, N.J. 08527. Catalogue 10¢
Far North Gardens, 15621 Auburndale Way, Livonia, Mich. 48154. (Seeds).
  Catalogue 25¢
Frank H. Rose, 1020 Poplar St., Missoula, Mont. 59801. (Seeds)
Gardens of the Blue Ridge, Ashford, McDowell City, N.C. 28603
Griffey's Nursery, Route 3, Box 17A, Marshall, N.C. 28753
Harry E. Saier, Dimondale, Mich. 48821. (Seeds). Catalogue 50¢
Highlands Nursery, Boxford, Mass. 01921
Jamieson Valley Gardens, Route 3B, Spokane, Wash. 99203. Catalogue $1.00
Lamb Nurseries, E. 101 Sharp Avenue, Spokane, Wash. 99202
Leslies Wildflower Nursery, 30 Summer St., Methuen, Mass. 01844. (Seeds).
  Catalogue 25¢
Midwest Wildflowers, Box 664A, Rockton, Ill. 61072. (Seeds). Catalogue 25¢
Nature's Garden, Route 1, Box 488, Beaverton, Ore. 97005. Catalogue 50¢
Orchid Gardens, Route 1, Grand Rapids, Minn. 55744. Catalogue 25¢
Pantfield Nurseries, Inc., 322 Southtown Road, Huntington, L.I., N.Y.
  11745
Putney Nursery, Putney, Vt. 05346. Catalogue 25¢

Siskiyou Rare Plant Nursery, 522 Franquette St., Medford, Ore. 97501.
   (Alpine and rock garden plants)
Sky-Cleft Gardens, Barre, Vt. 05641. (Shipped to U.S. only)
Thurman's Gardens, Route 2, Box 259, Spokane, Wash. 99200
The Wild Garden, 8243 N.E. 119th, Kirkland, Wash. 98033. Catalogue
   $1.00, deductible from order

Canada

Alpenglow Gardens, 13328 Trans-Canada Highway, North Surrey, New
   Westminster, B.C. (Mainly alpines). Catalogue 25¢
C. A. Cruickshank, Ltd., 1015 Mount Pleasant Road, Toronto, Ont. 315
Keith Somers, 10 Tillson Ave., Tillsonburg, Ont.

Index